NEVER PAY RETAIL CHICAGOLAND

Designer Merchandise at Discount Prices

Nona Mull Pickering

GuideLines

Cover Design and Graphics by *MERIDIAN CREATIVE GROUP*
Published by **GuideLines**

GuideLine books are available at special discounts for bulk
purchases for fund raisers or special promotions. Contact
GuideLines at P.O. Box 11051, Rockford, IL   61126-1051

Library of Congress Catalog Card Number: 91-90656
International Standard Book Number: 0-9631196-0-5

Dedicated

to my:

Father

Dan J Mull

for his undaunted spirit

and

Mother

Leola B. Mull

for her prudence and wisdom

Acknowledgements

Two years of my life, ten years worth of energy, and my lifetime clothing allowance have gone into this book. I could never have made it through each stage, let alone to completion, without the help of the following:

Research Assistance
Joan Blacklock
Nancy Bloomquist
Barbie Derby
Sue Hunting
Bob Pickering
Pat Pierceson
Nancy Walker

Technical Assistance
Bonnie Pauli
Rob Pickering

General Assistance
John Grigsby
Joan Papadopoulos

Editing Assistance
Lois Kramer

*A very special thank you
to my friend and consultant, Nancy Walker,
for her expertise;
to my sister, Nancy, for her inspiration;
to my two sons, Rob and D. J, for their
patience and encouragement;
and especially
to my husband, Bob, for his
optimism and support.*

Dear Fellow Shopper,

I've always been clothes conscious. My part-time job in high school was in retail, at Henry's, an upscale store in Wichita, Kansas where I grew up. I started learning about designers, style, fashion and trends at an early age. This retail learning experience continued at Saks Fifth Avenue where I worked while attending college at the University of Michigan. Then, after marrying, receiving a degree, teaching for three years, and having two children, I began sewing for the family. Working and teaching for Stretch and Sew, I learned about fabric and construction and most importantly, I learned how to design patterns which allowed me to be creative. I sewed for everyone - husband (including three piece suits), two young sons, sister, mother, father, etc. In two years my sewing machine burned up and so did my desire to use it.

Re-entering the retail market, I was both shocked at prices and aghast at the lack of quality. Labels I had previously worn and grown up with were amazingly expensive, and what I could afford was depressingly unimaginative,poorly constructed, and usually of inferior fabric. I wanted the best, but didn't want to pay retail. The answer - I became a shopper!

Actually I think I'd always been a shopper, the behavioral characteristics simply were dormant for a time. I started in earnest when we moved to Charleston, WV. The town had some incredibly small, exclusive, well stocked stores - and I shopped their sales. Not just the regular mark-down sales (although that's when I'd identify the merchandise I was really interested in, try it on, check the construction, etc.), but the really big sales held usually twice a year - the 75% off sales. I'd be the first in the door, and most of the time I'd already know what I wanted and that it fit, but then I'd find stuff for others, or for gifts. I found I really enjoyed this type of shopping - the dry mouth, the rapidly beating heart, the delight of discovering designer merchandise at incredibly good prices.

Apparel shopping, however, wasn't enough. We had built two homes by this time, and lived in several others, so I was definitely into furniture, accessories, and interior design. I accepted a part time job as receptionist/manager in an exclusive design shop and continued learning as well as spending every cent of my salary but at discount prices. In short I was doing well fulfilling my best for less desires, but then we moved again!

This time it was small city, U.S.A. and what I learned now were techniques for discovering upscale discount stores in nearby cities. I also shopped by phone, North Carolina for instance, and by plane, visiting friends who delighted in wrapping odd shaped packages for the plane ride home! In short, I went to great lengths to continue the type of shopping I enjoy. Yes, by this time I could have paid full price and gotten what I wanted, albeit not in as great a quantity or as often! I, however, like the challenge, get tired of most clothes after a couple of seasons, and believe in recycling and in bolstering the economy! Besides, and most importantly, it makes me smile!

We now live in Rockford, IL near one of the greatest cities in the world - Chicago! Talk about challenge and adventure! I started keeping a file of my discoveries and slowly an idea formed and a shopping guide evolved. I certainly don't claim to know all there is to know about Chicago - its architecture, historical sites and landmarks - as might a native; or to know every restaurant, be it ethnic, gourmet, or novelle cuisine, but I have made some wonderful discoveries in the apparel and home furnishing areas and I'm willing to share them with you. I hope **Never Pay Retail** leads you on adventures as enjoyable and as profitable as the ones I've had while compiling it!

Keep Smiling,
Nona

TABLE OF CONTENTS

WOMEN'S & MEN'S APPAREL

Anko Also

Lakeside Marketplace   Lighthouse Place
(See: Outlet Malls)   (See: Outlet Malls)

Anko Also typically carries lovely, drapey, flowing knits for women in solid colors. Some pieces, we were told, designed strictly for the outlets. Bargain Hunters should note the Back Rack of items where additional markdowns are taken each week. The merchandise on this rack is "clearance" and "as is" so check carefully. Items in the $300-$400 range are marked down $40 per week and items under $50 are marked down $5 per week.
See Also: Fashion Accessories

Ann Taylor Clearance Center

Gurnee Mills
(See: Outlet Malls)

Located in the huge, new, S-shaped, Gurnee Mills Outlet Mall, in number 735 at the bottom of the S, is the Ann Taylor Clearance Center, the only one in the midwest! Even in the hectic opening days the sales personnel were helpful, patient, and informative. The selection of current, sophisticated, stylish garments for women was excellent, and the prices, especially during the summer sale, were absolutely terrific. The store was busy and there was a wait for those who bothered to use the dressing rooms!

Anne Klein Outlet

Lakeside Marketplace   Lighthouse Place
(See: Outlet Malls)   (See: Outlet Malls)

Anne Klein carries current season women's apparel, accessories, and some Donna Karan seconds and samples. Merchandise moves from the front of the store where it is generally 30% off retail to the back of the store where real bargains can be found at 50% off the ticketed price. At a rack in the middle

2

of the store was a stunning red silk coat dress with a navy suede belt. Marked regularly at $300.00, the outlet price was $200.00 which had been reduced to $150.00 and then specially priced at 25% off the $150.00 ticketed price. In general we found the merchandise superb, the saleswomen friendly and helpful, and the bargains galore! As in most of the Lakeside stores there was a mailing list sign up sheet - we signed !
See Also: Fashion Accessories

Apparel Center Shops
350 N. Orleans Street
Chicago, IL 60654
M-F 9-5   Weekend hours vary

The Apparel Center is an interesting place to visit and a few of the rooms on the lower levels are open to the public. We "cased" the sample stores then enjoyed breakfast in the coffee shop eavesdropping on the various "trade" conversations until the opening hour of 9:00 AM. The first boutique we visited was **I. B. Diffusion** located in the lower level. It was relatively small, well stocked with current merchandise, and although there were sales on particular items, we were informed that it was essentially a retail store that had periodic sales - generally best before Christmas and in the summer. For lower all around prices shop the outlet store (See: **I. B. Diffusion,** page 16).

Next we visited **Arbetman & Goldbug Inc.,** a "wholesale distributor of men's European clothing & sportswear", located near I. B. Diffusion in the lower level. Their plentiful, current merchandise was color coded and the discount varied as to color. There is a chart on the wall explaining the code. The aggressive salesman hinted at possible further discounts, but we were satisfied with the designer socks we purchased on that particular visit.

Other stores open to the public on this level are **Silk Ltd.** with beautiful fabrics and **A. N. A. &**

Company with gorgeous dresses and suits. The upper levels of the Center, according to the posted signs, are closed to the public. However, just because we're curious we noted that the 5th floor is Bridal, the 6th Children's Wear/Maternity, the 7th & 8th Men's Wear, the 9th Accessories, the 11th Women's Sportswear/Dresses and the 12th & 13th Women's Better Apparel.

Bagatelle Factory Outlet
70 E. Randolph
Chicago, IL 60601
(312) 372-0909
M-F 9:30-7   Sat. 10-5:30

Bagatelle, a Canadian manufacturer, recently opened two retail stores in the Chicago area. The main store is located on Oak St. The other, an outlet, is on Randolph. At the time of our visit, two months after the opening, the outlet was having an inventory clearance sale. They carry upscale, contemporary styles for women in wool, leather and suede. A beautiful English Lamb Swing coat regularly $795 was $495; wool coats regularly $595 were $228. Besides the Bagatelle label we also saw Mondi. Hopefully the move to retail will be successful for Bagatelle, as we'd like to return, especially for the leather goods!

Brands Fashion Factory Outlets
Lakeside Marketplace   Lighthouse Place
(See: Outlet Malls)   (See: Outlet Malls)
(414) 857-9851

Brands, which carries apparel for men and women, is a collection of 31 select vendors (factory outlets) under one roof. Some of the name brands and designers noted were Leon Levin, Lakeland, Perry Ellis, Polo University Club, Pirelli by Superga, Mighty Mac and Sebago. The merchandise is

4

current, seasonal, and first quality. There are informative signs over the various groupings which indicate fabric content as well as other information about the garments including price: retail and Brand's (the garments are also tagged). Alterations are available and most can be completed the same day. This store is a fairly recent addition to Lakeside. The "mother store" is at Lighthouse Place in Michigan City.
See Also: Footwear

Burlington Coat Factory Warehouse
Talisman Center
Golf Rd. & Washington St. Harlem & Foster Aves.
Glenview, IL Chicago, IL
(708) 998-3440 (312) 763-6006

Lincoln Hwy & Crawford Barrington & Irving Pk.
Matteson, IL Hanover Park, IL
(708) 748-9393 (708) 213-7600

So. Cicero & 84th St. Villa Oaks Shop'g Ctr.
Burbank, IL Villa Park, IL
(708) 636-8300 (708) 832-4500

Arlington Plaza 920 Milwaukee Ave.
Arlington Hts, IL Libertyville, IL
(708) 577-7878

Century Consumer Mall
Merrillville, Ind
(219) 736-0636

Hours vary as to location.

Burlington Coat Factory carries name brand and some designer apparel for men, women and children at discounts that range from 25% to 60%. Labels include Liz Claiborne, Evan Picone, and others you'll recognize. Merchandise is current season, first quality and includes sportswear,

5

daywear, and eveningwear, besides the huge selection of outerwear.
See Also: Children's Apparel, Footwear, Linens

Buy-a-Tux
615 Roosevelt Rd.
Chicago, IL
(312) 243-5465
M-Sat. 10-6   Sun. 10-5

If you're in need of a tux, check them out at this location. They advertise the "largest selection of formal wear accessories anywhere" in addition to having "famous designer tuxedos at discount prices". The prices range from $329 to approximately $550. Don't miss the other River West stores at the plaza down the street or **Chernin's** directly across!

Calvin Klein
Lakeside Marketplace
(See: Outlet Malls)

We found Calvin Klein at Lakeside to be a large, well stocked, easy to shop store. It has a good selection of men's and women's apparel which appears to move quickly. The bright golden yellow T-Shirt I should have bought was no where to be seen on my next visit a couple of weeks later. Special seasonal sales can mean an additional 25% to 33% off the outlet price.

Cambridge Dry Goods Company, Inc.
Lakeside Marketplace
(See: Outlet Malls)
If you like the Cambridge style of mixed patterns, preppy, traditional sportswear, you'll love their outlet. We do and we found this store to be well organized with a good selection of women's apparel and helpful personnel. The lowest prices are on the

6

"as is" merchandise found on a table in the back of the shop and on sample items not chosen to be part of the line. I purchased a black cotton cardigan which was outlined in gold hand stitching in the latter category for $19.95, and we both purchased the long sleeved, padded shoulder T-shirts on sale for $10.00.

Casual Corner Clearance Center
Town & Country Mall
445 E. Palatine (Palatine & Arlington Heights Rd.)
Arlington Heights, IL
(708) 577-5333
M-F 10-9 Sat. 10-6 Sun. 11-5

While Lord & Taylor's Clearance Center looks like a warehouse, Casual Corner's Clearance Center, also located in the Town & Country Mall, appears to be a regular store. There are displays, carpeted areas, individual dressing rooms and organized sales racks. It's easy to shop and is a great place for teenage gals with all the usual Casual Corner brands at great prices. They had a good selection of activewear and rows of colorful jackets for the approaching winter. Note, this center has current season merchandise.
See Also: Fashion Accessories

Chicago Fur Mart
Marriott Hotel (Galleria)
540 N. Michigan Ave.
Chicago, IL 60611
(312) 923-1900
M-Sat. 10-6

Located in the Chicago Marriott Hotel, the Chicago Fur Mart advertises fantastic prices on all kinds of fur - "Natural mink full length coats for $1295, reg. $5000, $1395 reg. $6000." "Finnish Raccoon Full Length Coats - $995 reg. $5000." Check it out.

Chicago Fur Outlet-"Home of the furry godmother"
777 W. Diversey Pkwy. (at Halsted Street)
Chicago, IL
(312) 348-3877
Open 7 days but hours vary with the seasons

The Chicago Fur Outlet carries approximately one half new and one half "prefurred" resale furs, specializing in unique, one-of-a-kind pieces. Besides a variety of coats and jackets, they had what they term "parafurnalia" or headbands, hats, ear muffs, etc. This is their eighth year in business and, at least the day we visited, they were quite busy - both selling and accepting coats on consignment. As a full-service furrier they offer alterations and repairs, cleaning and storage, and are members of the Associated Fur Industries of Chicago.

CMcE Ltd.
615 Sheridan Rd.
Lake Bluff, IL
(708) 615-0735
M-Sat. 9:30-5:30

Owned by Carol McElwain Epkins, CMcE sells coordinating women's sportswear and dresses from natural fabric. Their specialty is pre-washed cotton knit which means washable for those tired of dry cleaning bills. The lines are sold by trained consultants at home shows throughout the country. The consultants' samples are sent back after the sales season and sold at the outlet in Lake Bluff. Besides samples (sizes 2 to 20), merchandise includes fallouts or mistakes. The clothes are described as "classic with a flair." As well as clothes, the store sells fabric. If you're interested in ordering from the regular line for full price, the sample board is available and they'll take your order. Regular prices run $50 to $120; outlet prices are approximately half that amount.

8

Coat Rack
1900 Waukegan Rd.
Glenview, IL
(708) 729-2377

Fall M-F 10-9   Sat. 10-6   Sun. 11-5
Summer M, Th. 10-9   T,W,F,S 10-6   Sun. 12-5

To our delight the Coat Rack carries much more than coats, not that the coats aren't terrific - they are, but we also like the women's sportswear (Biz, Carole Little, Karen Kane), Hanes hosiery and the array of accessories including belts, scarfs, jewelry, and gloves.   Nancy W. found terrifically trendy, block multi-colored tights which she topped with a swinging A line, black knit mini.   Then we moved on to the coats, over 5,000 coats for men (38 to 46), women (2 to 20, 14 1/2 to 24 1/2), and girls (7 to 14). The merchandise is first quality and current. The selection varies.   They discount 15% to 20% and run sales every five to six weeks.

Dan Howard's Maternity Factory
The Annex
215 W. Golf Road
Schaumburg, IL
(708) 884-8990

320 E. Rand Road
Arlington Hgts, IL
(708) 398-2114

2413 N. Clark Street
Chicago, IL
(708) 969-4666

2019 Ogden Avenue
Downers Grove, IL
(708) 528-9600

16707 S. Torrence
Lansing, IL
(708) 895-8333

304 South Route 59
Naperville, IL
(708) 355-2004

9026 Milwaukee Avenue
Niles, IL
(708) 299-2800

7305 W. 25th Street
North Riverside, IL
(708) 447-2772

9535 S. Cicero Avenue
Oak Lawn, IL
(708) 423-5580

15024 La Grange Rd
Orland Park, IL
(708) 460-8778

701 N. Milwaukee Ave
Vernon Hills, IL
(708) 680-1200

3217 Lake Avenue
Wilmette, IL
(708) 251-3303

Hours vary as to location.

Dan Howard's Maternity Factory (the actual factory is located in Chicago) would rather not term itself an outlet stating instead that the stores offer lower prices (about 25% to 50% lower) by eliminating the middleman. There are numerous locations in the Chicago area and they offer a good selection of quality maternity clothes. Special sales are held periodically.

Eddie Bauer
Factory Outlet Centre
(See: Outlet Malls)
(414) 857-7061

As their slogan states, this men's and women's clothing outlet is "Real Eddie Bauer at unreal prices"! They carry firsts and seconds of overstocked and discontinued merchandise which is shipped weekly from their retail and catalog inventory. The savings run 30% to 70%. The store and the selection are large. Some labels we spotted in women's apparel other than Eddie Bauer were All Week Long and Susan Bristal.
See Also: Footwear, Fantastic Sales

Notable: Clothing for Tall Women
Several lines now carry a variety of clothing for ladies 5 feet 8 inches and taller, but if you want the convenience of a catalog, try Long Tall Sally; call (800) 966-TALL.

Eisenstein Clothing Co.
River West Plaza
555 Roosevelt
Chicago, IL
(312) 738-0028
M-S 9-4:30   Sun. 10-3

There are rows and rows of men's suits and sport coats and when we first visited, a special sale on top coats. Selection was good in all areas: size, fabric, and style. According to the salesman, the percentage off is approximately 50%. During our next visit, the ties caught my attention - two for the price of the most expensive. That meant two $60 ties for $36 and I, to my regret and my son's regret, didn't get them! The summer sale was on and a chart indicated the additional percentage off the suits and sport coats. Mr. "Bobby" Bauer was helpful, patient, and informative. I suggest parking in the Plaza parking lot and if you purchase something, remember to get your ticket validated.

Evan-Picone
Lakeside Marketplace
(See: Outlet Malls)

Evan-Picone carries a good selection of both women's and men's apparel, especially if you're looking for traditional tailored sportswear. We saw Austin Hill, Izod and Gant labels as well as Evan-Picone and at the time of our visit there was 50% off Trifari jewelry and Monet handbags.

Notable: Sporty Labels for Less
In June 1991 new secondary lines debuted for Ellen Tracey (Company), Anne Klein II (A Line - check out the controversial ad campaign), and Michael Kors (Kors). These lines are sportier and less expensive.

Fenn Wright & Manson
Lakeside Marketplace
(See: Outlet Malls)

Fenn Wright & Manson advertises "updated casual and career apparel for men and women". Their merchandise is current and first quality with the great majority constructed of natural fiber - cotton and silk. Items are discounted 40% to 60%, with special sale items for $5 and $10. During July approximately half of the merchandise is marked down to $10 as this is when the Fall line arrives. According to Joanne, a delightful sales clerk, stores which carry Fenn Wright & Manson clothes include Bloomingdale, Macy's and Lord & Taylor. They also manufacture clothes for the Gap and Casual Corner.

Filene's Basement
State and Madison   Gurnee Mills
Chicago, IL   (See: Outlet Malls)

One Schaumburg Place
Schaumburg, IL

Hours vary as to location.

Filene's Basement, the original off-price bargain basement, has arrived in the Chicago area! Headquartered in Boston, the basement of Filene's is famous throughout the Northeast for its specially priced men's and women's apparel. (Also check out children's clothes and footwear!) The merchandise comes from manufacturers' and designers' overruns, canceled orders, and buyouts from major stores - ever wonder what happens to the end-of-season clothes at Saks? The merchandise is current and labels include all of the familiar names such as Liz Claiborne, Evan-Picone, Perry Ellis, and Calvin Klein. Selection varies as in any off-price store.
See Also: Fashion Accessories, Fantastic Sales

14 Plus Pizazz
Lighthouse Place Outlet Center
(See: Outlet Malls)

14 Plus Pizazz is a locally owned store which carries larger sizes in women's apparel. Included in their name brands are Andrea Gayle, bonnie and bill by holly, Leslie Fay II and Alfred Dunner. The percentage off runs from 20% to 75% with items starting at 20% and then undergoing markdowns. There are on going sales and a big sidewalk sale the third week of August. They also carry some jewelry, hats and handbags.

Galt Sand
Lakeside Marketplace
(See: Outlet Malls)
(414) 857-7110

Galt Sand is a fun store filled with all the college logo sweats and T-shirts. Besides the college items, we noticed the Bloomie's Golf Classic T-Shirt for $9.80, regularly $14, and Saks Fifth Avenue World Championship Golf Classic T-shirt for $9.80, regularly $14. The Bargain Corner is in the back of the store, but as the sign states you're on your own here, there is no order to the items - check carefully. The discounts range from 30% to 70%.

Notable: Chicago Designers
Every year the Apparel Industry Board names Chicago's "Designer of the Year". The designer is chosen by a committee of fashion professionals; voted upon by retailers and members of the fashion industry. Winners of the coveted award include Becky Bisoulis, Hino & Malee, Maria Rodriquez, and Mark Heister.

Gentry

Danada Square West	Cross Roads Ctr.
138 Danada Square West	227 Skokie Valley
Wheaton, IL 60187	Highland Park, IL (708)
665-9700	(708) 831-7666
Arlington Towne Square	Webster Place Ctr
87 West Golf Rd	1445 W. WebsterAve
Arlington Heights, IL	Chicago, IL 60614
(708) 364-8111	(312) 528-6400

M-F 10-9:30   Sat. 10-6 (Webster Place 10-9:30)
Sun. 11-6

With more than a dozen giant stores in the Midwest, and with their own buyer in New York, the Gentry is advertised as the "leading off-price retailer of famous make and designer men's clothing." The stores are divided into two separate sections: one side for dress, including sport coats, suits, dress pants and top coats; and one side for men's furnishings and casual sweaters, shirts, jackets, and activewear. Because of direct competition in the immediate area, I was asked not to reveal designer labels, but you'll recognize them when you see them. The discount runs 30% to 60% less than the best regular price stores and there are tailors and fitters on the premises with at least the possibility of same day alterations. They have a hundred different suit sizes ranging to size 52 and accept all major charge cards.

Geoffrey Beene
Lakeside Marketplace
(See: Outlet Malls)

We're disappointed they're not carrying the women's line, but the men will be thrilled that the limited space is devoted entirely to them!

Harvé Benard
Lakeside Marketplace   Lighthouse Place
(See: Outlet Malls)   (See: Outlet Malls)

Harve Benard carries men's and women's apparel (traditionally tailored, pricey, executive type) and a limited selection of shoes, hats, jewelry and Harve Benard watches. Nancy took time to appreciate the attractively displayed, current, fall merchandise while I ran to the sale rack of silk separates - a good selection of pants, skirts, jackets, and tops in a variety of colors. The store is spacious, having expanded into space previously occupied by the Wool Shed, and shopping is a pleasure. As an additional plus, the women's dressing rooms open to a large, private "viewing room" with a three-way mirror - an arrangement that warrants an "A".

He-Ro Group Outlet
Gurnee Mills
(See: Outlet Malls)

We found beautiful, expensive clothes for women at He-Ro Group Outlet, formerly **Oleg Cassini European Collections.** The apparel ran the gamut from sportswear, including leather, to dresses and beautifully tailored suits, to eveningwear. The beaded pieces really caught our eye as there was a good selection - gowns, long and short, and some tops. They were beautiful and were in excellent condition as well! The "Group" includes such designers as Bill Blass, Palmer & Palmer and Bob Mackie. Again we recommend signing up for the mailing list.

Notable: Off-Price Chains
Some of the biggest off-price chains are: Marshalls, T.J. Maxx, Burlington, Loehmann's, Hit or Miss, Ross Stores, Syms, Filene's Basement, Designer Depot, and Clothestime.

I. B. Diffusion

Lakeside Marketplace   Lighthouse Place
(See: Outlet Malls)   (See: Outlet Malls)
(414) 857-9090

Apparel Center
350 N. Orleans Street
Chicago, IL 60654
170 Lower Level
M-F 9-5 Weekend hours vary

    I. B. Diffusion is known for its beading - on sweaters, blouses, jackets - you name it! The store carries merchandise for women that is first quality, some from past season (not marked, just ask if you care to find out), samples in size 8 (medium), and a selection of clothes in larger sizes. The discount starts at 30% except samples which are 50% off. Items that do not move continue to be marked down. The clearance rack is located in one of the back two corners.

Irv's Clothing

Palwaukee Plaza
610 Milwaukee Ave.   2841 N. Laramie
Prospect Heights, IL   Chicago, IL 60641
(708) 459-8060   (312) 286-7293

7511 Lemont Road
Darien, IL 60559
(708) 910-1333

M-F 10-9   Sat. & Sun. 10-5

    Located, as they say, "in three inconvenient locations", Irv's men's clothing offers a wide selection of current season, first quality designerwear. Included are suits, sport coats, pants, shirts, sportswear, outerwear, accessories and even shoes. Everything for the discriminating male. Labels include Halston, Pierre Cardin, Givenchy,

Botany 500, Bill Blass, Perry Ellis, and Chaps by Ralph Lauren. A gorgeous, 100% cashmere, black top coat we noticed was priced at $500. A 100% wool, Bill Blass sport coat was $160. As can well be expected, the store was busy. Sales personnel were plentiful, helpful, and friendly.

J. Crew Factory Store
Lakeside Marketplace
(See: Outlet Malls)

If you love the catalog, you'll like the outlet. The traditional, yet brightly colored sportswear for men and women really appeals to my eighteen year old and I've been careful to keep him away! I did, however, buy him a braided natural leather belt for 30% off their outlet price of $18.95. The end-of-season sales are terrific here if you can wait until July or February.

J.H. Collectibles Factory Outlet
Lakeside Marketplace   Lighthouse Place
(See: Outlet Malls)   (See: Outlet Malls)

J.H. Collectibles carries a really nice selection of high quality women's apparel, including petites. Although pricey, there are definitely savings to be made. Nancy spotted a red, swing coat, regularly priced at $250.00 on a special sale for $139.99! The store is spacious, having expanded into the space previously occupied by That's Our Bag, thus a pleasure in which to shop.

Jindo
Lakeside Marketplace   Lighthouse Place
(See: Outlet Malls)   (See: Outlet Malls)

Boardwalk Shop'g Mall   Northbrook Court
4140 Dempster St.   1500 Lake Cook Dr.
Skokie, IL 60076   Northbrook, IL

While the largest "mother store" of the region is located on Dempster in Skokie with the factory, the Jindo store at Lakeside has plenty of luscious, soft, beautiful furs. According to the manager, Jindo is not only the largest manufacturer of fur, but also the best! They carry a variety of styles and types of fur with a large selection of mink, and their sales personnel is very helpful, especially for those who want to learn about fur. They run daily specials.

Jonathan Logan
Factory Outlet Centre   Lighthouse Place
(See: Outlet Malls)   (See: Outlet Malls)

Besides the obvious Jonathan Logan, we spotted women's clothes with all of the following labels: Village Petites, Rafaella, E.D. Michaels Petites, Jessica Howard, Jackie & Eric Ltd., and CC Magic by Toni. The latter was a quilted long sleeved jacket on a "new arrival" rack. It was regularly priced at $105.00 and outlet priced at $69.99. The merchandise included in the end-of-season sale was an additional 25% to 50% off. Accessories included earrings by Encore.

Jones NY Factory Store
Lakeside Marketplace
(See: Outlet Malls)

We loved Jones NY Factory Store. The Christian Dior current fall outfits, especially the black and white grouping, were dynamite! The store also carries Seville as well as the Jones New York and JonesWear labels. There was a good selection of petites and three racks where the second piece of equal or less value could be obtained for $10.00. A great place for women's apparel!

18

Lands' End Outlet
2241 & 2317 North Elston Ave
(Exit E. off I- 94 onto Fullerton,
turn S. on Elston)
Chicago, IL
(312) 276-2232 & 384-4170

Yorkshire Plaza
Fox Valley,IL
(708)851-2990

Yorktown Convenience Center
Butterfield & Highland
Lombard,IL
(708)953-8855

6131 W. Dempster
Morton Grove, IL
(708)470-0320

Lake View Plaza
159th & LaGrange Rd.
Morton Grove, IL
(708)403-2020

The Annex
251 W. Golf Rd.
Schaumburg, IL
(708)884-1900

8161/2 Church Street
Evanston, IL
(708) 328-3009

Hours vary as to location.

Lands' End has several outlets in the greater Chicago area and while the ones on Elston don't claim to be the biggest or best, just the original, we sure enjoyed shopping both the women's store (2317 N. Elston Ave) and the men's store (2241 N. Elston Ave).   Enter their parking lot by driving between the chain link fences, then use the "parking lot" to drive between stores - Elston gets pretty busy during rush hours and you're close to an entrance to I-94/90. Once inside it took us awhile to figure out their mark down system - you'll have a head start! Besides first quality catalog overstocks and end-of-season merchandise, the stores also have returned items and seconds (quality not up to standard). Clothes in the latter category come to the stores at 40% off the original catalog price, are marked with a green tag, and are marked down on a regular basis up to an additional 75% off the first 40% . A chart on the wall in the "green tag area" will help you determine how far the item has been marked down. Real bargains abound in this area if you can remove the monogram, get out the spot, or otherwise correct or live with the flaw. The first quality merchandise (blue tags) starts at 20% off the original price. Weekly specials are terrific. (A special note - two of the stores, Evanston, IL. and Madison, WI, carry only "Not Quite Perfect" merchandise.) Special thanks to Thelma, a terrific sales associate, for all her help! Note - other locations carry both women's and men's apparel.

Liesl's Sample Shop
6970 N. Sheridan Rd.
Chicago, IL 60626
(312) 764-1130
W-F 11-6 Sat. 11-5 Closed M,T and Sun.

Linda and Angela now own Liesl's Sample Shop which sells apparel for women. They do the buying locally, only have one of each item, and never carry items from season to season. Labels include A.K.A, Revolution, and Fizz silks. The everyday discount is 25% to 30% and during sales 50% to 75%. While samples run from size 4 to 12, many items aren't marked. Be sure to try on and check items carefully. Nancy found a cotton knit shorts outfit for the Buick Open and I found an off white cotton stretch pant and top ($40, but the elastic needed work). We're pleased, especially with the friendly atmosphere and personal attention! Street parking.

Notable: Museum Stores
When visiting the various museums in town, a must when "doing" Chicago, don't forget there are shops in each museum! Wonderful unique, exotic treasures can be found. The Art Institute even has a satellite shop at 900 N. Michigan Ave.

Liz Claiborne Outlet Store
Lakeside Marketplace
(See: Outlet Malls)

The Liz Claiborne Outlet Store carries women's and men's apparel - discontinued, leftovers, odd lots and overruns, and accessories. It is a large store with lots of merchandise which, when busy, can make it crowded and difficult to shop. The selection, however, is grand and includes the various Claiborne labels as well as Dana Buchman. Look for the specially priced racks. We noticed a beautiful, yellow linen, short sleeved blouse regularly priced at $62.00 for $29.99.
See Also: Fashion Accessories

Loehmann's
Village Plaza
Dempster & Harlem
Morton Grove, IL
(708) 966-1350

Loehmann's Plaza
320 East Golf Rd
Arlington Hgts, IL
(708) 228-5570

Finley Square Mall
Downers Grove, IL

Matteson Town Center
Matteson, IL

Hours vary as to location.

Loehmann's is one of the original designer off-price stores and is definitely one of our favorites for women's apparel. They carry top quality designer and name brand clothing, most often with the label removed, ranging from activewear to formalwear including suede, leather and cashmere. For the top designers and couture items look in the Back Room, located, where else, in the back of the store. Be prepared to leave your selections from the main room on a clothes rack outside the door and to try on clothes in the Back Room itself if you happen to be in a strict store that doesn't allow Back Room clothes to leave the room. (There are "community" type dressing rooms available for use with main room

21

clothes.) My latest purchase from the Back Room is a purple silk, long sleeved dress with marvelous off set brass buttons - a Bill Blass for, would you believe, $89.99! During this visit we also noticed beaded tops for $59 and up and beaded gowns for $199 and up. Select your purchases carefully. Return policies have recently been implemented and items may be returned for store credit. In the Chicago area the largest store with the best selection is in Morton Grove.
See Also: Fashion Accessories

Lord & Taylor Clearance Center
Town & Country Mall
445 E. Palatine (Palatine and Arlington Hts. Rd.)
Arlington Heights, IL
(708) 259-4211
M-F 10-9 Sat. 10-6 Sun .11-5

Lord and Taylor operates three clearance centers around the country, one of them in Arlington Heights in the Town & Country Mall. This center receives past season merchandise from numerous stores in this general section of the country. The clothes are at least 35% off the last marked down price, and Thursday through Monday there are various racks marked down as much as 60%. The store, which carries women's, men's and children's apparel, as well as some accessories, handbags, lingerie, and outerwear, is organized according to departments. In other words there are numbers on the racks which relate to the department the clothes come from and recently, the name of the designer - and that's it! From that point on, it's up to you! If you're not in the mood to really "shop", save this center for another day. For instance, my boys "looked over" the men's department in approximately 15 minutes, said it had nothing, and promptly left for Woodfield Mall! When they returned, about an hour and a half later, I showed

them the Perry Ellis cardigan sweater I'd found -$34 from $120. They loved it and their grandfather did too when he received it for Christmas! This kind of shopping, ladies and gentlemen, is a JOB! It definitely takes more time as you have to search for sizes, to check for faults, and to simply cover the vast array of merchandise. It helps to know that the highest priced designers (Anne Klein, Ralph Lauren, etc.) are located in front of the cash registers as you enter with the "medium" priced designers (Liz Claiborne, J. G. Hook, etc.) located to the left. The petite section is behind that, lingerie is located in the back usually on the left, and dresses are in the back toward the middle. Men's apparel is to the right as you enter the store and children's clothes are in the back generally to the right. (Unless, of course, they change it all!) Luckily there are dressing rooms and rest rooms! If one is mentally prepared and physically comfortable - especially shoes - this clearance center can be the best bargain opportunity around! It's a challenge and we love it!! The mall offers other opportunities for bargains including the **Casual Corner Clearance Center.** Doing both on the same day, however, could classify one as masochistic!
See Also: Children's Apparel, Lingerie, Fashion Accessories

Manhattan Factory Outlet
Factory Outlet Centre   Lighthouse Place
(See: Outlet Malls)   (See: Outlet Malls)

410 South First St.
St. Charles, IL
(312) 377-2162

Hours vary as to location.

Manhattan Factory Stores is a division of Manhattan Industries, Inc. so each store carries not only items with the Manhattan label as you would

23

expect, but also men's and women's sportswear with labels which include Perry Ellis, Anne Klein, Henry Grethel, and John Henry. We also noticed Vera accessories. The savings are up to 60%, possibly more at the end-of-season closeouts. Be sure to ask about their frequent buyer's club.

Mark Shale Outlet
2593 North Elston
(north from Fullerton, in a small mall with Cub Food; large parking lot)
Chicago, IL 60647
(312) 772-9600
M-F 10-8   Sat. 10-6   Sun. 12-5

Whoa! Wait a minute! This may be a wrong turn as far as finding Land's End, but isn't that a Mark Shale Outlet in the corner of this small Cub Food mall? Visions of beautiful, current, traditional, upscale clothing danced in my head and I was not disappointed. As of our visit this was Mark Shale's only outlet. Ten of their retail stores ship end-of-season remainders, overstocks and other odds and ends here and they're marked from 30% to 70% below original retail. There was an extensive selection of Polo-Ralph Lauren for both men and women, and I fell in love with a particular 100% white linen, double breasted blazer with brass buttons. It was $149 from $375. In general we were both impressed by the selection of women's sportswear and dresses, but the men's selection of suits, sport coats and sportswear is even greater! We noticed in the men's shirts that imperfections, when present, are tagged and the location is identified. If it doesn't fit, they offer alterations, and if you're too busy to shop, they'll take your order by phone and mail it to you! Ask to be notified of their special sales. To complete the rosy picture is their motto, "No sale is final until you are completely satisfied." Definitely not a wrong turn!

Marshalls
The following store is the largest:
95th & Cicero (294 South, exit 95th St. east)
Oaklawn, IL
(708) 424-8388

Call 1-800-MARSHAL for the one nearest you.
Hours vary as to location.

With over 375 stores nationwide Marshalls is as familiar as apple pie. It's also easy to shop with the items you're probably looking for in the designer section up front in both the women's and the men's section.   I always run back and check linens and shoes - you never can tell. The store listed does the largest volume sales in the Chicago area thus is considered the largest.
See Also: Children's Apparel, Fashion Accessories, Housewares

Mondi
Gurnee Mills
(See: Outlet Malls)

European, Current, High Style, Expensive! These women's clothes remind us of Chicago's Oak Street or Henri Bendel's windows on Michigan Ave. Beautiful clothes for the clothes conscious - here at discounted prices!

Morris & Sons Co.
River West Plaza
555 W. Roosevelt Road
Chicago, IL 60607
(312) 243-5635
M-Sat. 9-5:30 Sun. 9-4

555 W. Roosevelt Road turned out to be a mini shopping center with Morris & Sons Co. located, as they say, at the "top 'o' the Bank". We climbed the

stairs, rang the bell, and were buzzed in. The store carries men's and women's high fashion, designer, and some couture clothing as well as a few pairs of men's shoes and a smattering of accessories. The clothes were beautiful and even at 30% off retail, expensive. Nancy, however, persevered and found the buy of the day! A stunning, yellow cotton LECrillon on a special summer sale for 50% off marked price which made it $75.00. She had seen the dress on a gal in Palm Beach that past winter. Bob, meanwhile, was busy trying on Brioni suits. Originally priced at $2200.00, these suits were marked around $900.00 with a special buy out rack for $600.00. Obviously the seasonal sale racks and various promotions yield the best buys. Be sure to ask how you can get on their mailing list and be notified of their once a year private sale. Although they do not offer alterations, there is a tailor located in a shop across the hall.
See Also: Children's Apparel

Nike Factory Outlet
Until December 1991   After December 1991
12225 71st Street   Lakeside Marketplace
Kenosha, WI 53142   (See: Outlet Malls)
(414) 857-7333

The Nike Factory Outlet located across Hwy 50 from the Factory Outlet Centre is large and fully packed. They offer a wide range of sports apparel as well as footwear for men, women and children. Their markdown is approximately 30% to 40%, with special sales the week of July 4th and Labor Day.
See Also: Children's Apparel, Footwear

931 West
931 W. Belmont Ave.
Chicago, IL 60657
(312) 549-1500
M-F 11-7 Sat.10-6 Sun. 12-5

931 West is a boutique which carries current, contemporary, upscale women's fashions at 30% to 50% off. According to the salesperson, most of the merchandise is from New York. Blazers regularly $149 to $199 were priced at $98. Labels I noticed were Et Vous, a.b.s, and Girbaud (several pairs of jeans). The shop is worth it, but the traffic and parking, especially on Saturday, can be a real problem.

Off Center Building
300 W. Grand Ave.
Chicago, IL 60601
Hours vary as to location

The Off Center Building in River North at 300 W. Grand Ave. houses some interesting outlet stores. **Christine** in Suite 610, (312) 644-3021, M-F 10-5 or by appointment, has women's apparel and accessories by Chicago designer Christine Goldschmidt at 50% to 70% off. Nancy discovered the perfect skirt with a choice of two jackets from the couture line which ran $350 an outfit. The separates from a secondary line were less expensive running $40 to $70 each. Prices were not marked on the items, but the salesperson was patient and answered all our questions! The clothes were unique, stylish, and well made.

Another interesting store in this building is **Fun With Furs**, an exclusive manufacturer of pillows, rugs, bedspreads and apparel in fur. Their hours are by appointment (312) 670-2442 and prices are 50% off the marked price.

Other outlets appear to come and go at this location so check the directory and ask the friendly security guard as you enter.
See Also: Fashion Accessories

Oshkosh B'Gosh
Lakeside Marketplace
(See: Outlet Malls)

Oshkosh B'Gosh The Genuine Article carries some women's, some men's and mostly children's apparel as well as a number of accessories including socks, hats, purses, and diaper bags. The regular retail price was not marked, but I was told that discounts range from 20% to 50%. Sale items were marked with a red sticker and an additional percentage was taken off at the register. The men's bib overalls were $22.55 and the prerequisite bandana was $1.00. The store was spacious and well laid out.
See Also: Children's Apparel

Otiswear
1971 N. Halsted
Chicago, IL
(312) 943-5151
M-W 11-7   Th 11-8   F 11-6   Sat. 10-6   Sun. 12-5

Otiswear is a manufacturer's outlet featuring 100% cotton knitwear for women and children. The cotton is mostly double ply which means it's that nice heavier weight. Attractive styles abound! The discount is 20% with sale items reduced 40% to 70%. The jewelry was interesting with some unique, special pieces at 20% off.
See Also: Children's Apparel

Polo - Ralph Lauren
Lighthouse Place
(See: Outlet Malls)
(219) 874-9442

I am always excited about seeing and shopping the Polo-Ralph Lauren outlet at Lighthouse Place and apparently everyone else is too as the store always seems quite busy, especially during seasonal sales. It handles men's, women's, and some children's apparel, footwear, and linens. On our visits the selection in all areas has always been good. They carry first quality and irregulars so watch the signs and tags. The irregular knits, short sleeved traditional and long and short sleeved T-shirts, were priced at $23.99 (1st quality $34.99), while some irregular Rugbys were $39.99 (1st quality $59.99). There was also a special sale rack marked women's clearance $9.99 to $99.99. Special note must be made of the attractive displays in the windows and around the store which simply emphasize the quality to be found within. Also adding to the pleasure of the visit was the helpfulness of the clerks even amid the bustling crowd. Unfortunately they no longer take phone orders because of competition with their regular retail stores.

See Also: Children's Apparel, Footwear, Linens

Rainbow Fashions
Factory Outlet Centre
(See: Outlet Malls)
(414) 857-7666

Rainbow Fashions, which carries women's apparel, is billed as The Sportswear Store and that it is. We found the selection to be especially good for Juniors. Bugle Boy, Bonjour and Jordache jeans for $19.95, valued at $35-$40, Hang Ten separates at 50% off, and a wide assortment of colored crew socks for 99 cents.

Royal Robbins
Lakeside Marketplace
(See: Outlet Malls)
(414) 857-9496

Royal Robbins carries casual men's and women's clothing "with outdoor spirit" of natural fibers and dyeing such as pigment dyed sand cloth. The clothes are mostly firsts which start at 35% off retail. The seconds are immediately marked at wholesale. There are periodic sales, for instance Labor Day and Memorial Day weekends. Comparison shoppers can find the Royal Robbins' clothes at Erehwon. (NO WHERE spelled backwards!) I was told that they will take phone orders and will ship.

Sagrani   Clothiers
Marriott Galleria (Shop No. 210)
Marriott Hotel
540 N. Michigan Ave
Chicago, IL 60611
(312) 644-0604
M-F 10-6:30 Sat 10-6

Sagrani Clothiers, located in the Galleria of the Marriott Hotel just down from the Chicago Fur Mart, carries a good selection of men's apparel. They advertise brand name suits at discount prices including Givenchy, Halston, Alexander Julian, Chap's by Ralph Lauren, and Valentino. Italian silk ties were priced at $19.90 the day we visited, and they had fine wool V-neck and turtleneck sweaters in four or five colors for $65. If you can't find what you need, they also custom make clothes.

Notable: In Search of the Best Prices
The absolute best prices are always off season at clearance sales when you can get 75% to 90% off retail. This eventually happens at a few department stores, some exclusive shops, at outlets, off-price stores, and clearance centers. To find out where and when this will happen, you can continuously scope out the territory, make a friend amongst the sales staff, or peruse the newspaper for special clearance sales. After you've discovered where to be and at what time, remember: Buy it when you See it to Have it when you Need it!

Spiegel Outlet Stores

1105 W. 35th St.
Chicago, IL

9950 Joliet Rd.
Countryside, IL

220 S. Waukegan Rd.
Deerfield, IL

1432 Butterfield Rd.
Downers Grove, IL

540 S. Route 59
Naperville, IL

4 Orland Park Pl.
Orland Park, IL

1331 N. Rand Rd.
Palatine, IL

200 E. North Ave.
Villa Park, IL

Gurnee Mills
(See: Outlet Malls)

Hours vary as to location.

The Spiegel Outlet Stores have everything - from women's, men's, and children's apparel, footwear, and accessories to furniture and all types of housewares - and there are several of them in the Chicago area. During one visit there was a special coat sale with outlet prices marked 50% off the original catalog price. During another, selected dresses were specially priced. The women's apparel included such labels as Donna Karan New York (DKNY), J.H. Collectibles, and Liz Claiborne. The atmosphere was as pleasant as the prices with attractive displays, soft music, and ample space to move around.

See Also: Children's Apparel, Lingerie, Fashion Accessories, Footwear, Furniture, Housewares, Linens

---

Notable: Off-Price Stores
As a result of buying in high volume, purchasing overruns, canceled orders and sometimes past-season goods, and taking less of a mark-up, off-price stores can sell merchandise at decidedly lower prices than department stores.

Sportique Fashion Outlet
4200 W. Belmont Ave.
Chicago, IL
(312) 685-9577

Closed M,T, W Open Thurs. & Fri. 8:30-9:30
Sat. 8:30-7:30 Sun. 10-6:30

Sportique Fashion Outlet advertises "current brand name and designer fashions for misses, juniors, and plus-sizes at discount prices." Labels we noted were Palmetto's, S.B. Sport, S.K and Company, Norton McNaughton, MyMichelle, Razzle Me, and Forenza. We were impressed, especially for juniors and cost conscious parents. A really good looking two piece, 100% cotton plaid shirt and skirt outfit with interesting detailing was only $20 or $9.99 each piece. They receive new merchandise every week, sometimes twice a week, but please note the hours and the fact that they are closed Mon, Tues and Wed.

Sportmart
Schaumburg
1015 E. Golf Rd
Schaumburg, IL
(708) 517-7701

River North
440 N. Orleans St
Chicago, IL
(312) 222-0900

Lakeview
3100 N. Clark Street
Chicago, IL
(312) 871-8501

Bricktown
6420 Fullerton Ave.
Chicago, IL
(312) 804-0044

Rt. 59 & E. New York Ave.
Fox Valley, IL
(708) 851-8890

1500 S. Harlem Ave.
North Riverside, IL
(708) 366-6600

1385 Orland Park Place
Orland Park, IL
(708) 460-0900

9633 S. Cicero Ave
Oak Lawn, IL
(708) 636-0501

1500 S. Torrence Ave.
Calumet City, IL
(708) 895-0901

255 Roosevelt Road
Lombard, IL
(708) 620-0901

240 E. Dundee Road
Wheeling, IL
(708) 520-4321

7233 W. Dempster St
Niles, IL
(708) 967-7601

Hours vary as to location.

Sportmart is a discount chain with numerous stores in the Chicago area. They carry all manner of sports apparel for men, women, and children, and advertise "name brands for less everyday". They had the Coolsport Coordinates for women - $28.98 for pants and $27.96 for the top with a built in bra. We also noted a Columbia jacket within a shell (red with two tone blue) for $159.96. They carry NFL official licensed products, as well as various sports equipment and athletic shoes.
See Also: Children's Apparel, Footwear

Studio 90
5239 North Clark St.
Chicago, IL
(312) 878-0097
T-F 11-7   S & S 11-5   Closed Mon.

Studio 90 is a treat! The clothes are cotton, simplistic, and flattering. In their new location on Clark St., Jill Hilgenberg and and her partner, Angela Turley, display their women's clothes at the front of the store and cut out new ones in the rear. The counter with the cash register separates the two areas. Prices are fantastic - only slightly above their wholesale prices to Oak Street and Water Tower Place stores. For instance, short, cotton jackets are priced at $48; pants at $39. If you can't find your size in the item you want (sizes are 1,2, and 3), then take advantage of what they term "participatory buying". Choose fabric from the bolts on hand and

33

they'll have it made up and shipped to you. New fabric comes in every two weeks or so and items move quickly. Nancy B. has been complimented so often on her outfit that she's sending me back to choose another for her!

T. H. Mandy

659 W. Diversey Pkwy
Chicago,IL 60614
(312) 975-1800

1330 Butterfield Rd.
Downers Grove, IL
(708) 953-1771

Downer's Grove, IL
708) 241-1070

Bloomingdale, IL
(708) 980-1060

Vernon Hills, IL
(708) 816-6700

Chicago Ridge.IL
(708) 499-4343

225 N. Michigan Avenue
Chicago, IL
(312) 938-4300

Deerfield, IL
(708) 940-8400

Skokie's Fashion Square
Skokie, IL
(708) 675-6647

Meadowstown Mall
(708) 228-7886

Arlington Heights, IL
(708) 632-1050

Hours vary as to location.

The T.H. Mandy store on Diversey Pkwy. is across the street from Private Lives, one of our favorite linen stores, so if you are so lucky as to find a parking place in this ultra busy section of Lincoln Park, be sure to visit both! Besides the women's sportswear, appealing especially to teens (J.H.Collectibles, Kasper, Cherokee, Sportswear Systems) the store also carries a large selection of accessories.
See Also: Fashion Accessories

T. J. Maxx
There are numerous locations.
The following are two of the largest:

135 Skokie Hwy   7250 Dempster
Highland Park, IL   Morton Grove, IL
(708) 831-1500   (708) 966-4483

Hours vary as to location.

The "Maxx for the Minimum". It's a slogan as familiar to discount shoppers as that of McDonald's is to fast food eaters. There are designer names among the brand names if the store is not one of the ones that groups them separately. At one location an Ellen Tracy silk jacket could be purchased for $100 plus the ability to chase a forgotten, tiny sticker which was lodged between the jacket and lining, down to the hem where it would not be visible. All is not imperfect, just check to be sure. Check also the linen and houseware sections for possible surprises.
See Also: Children's Apparel, Fashion Accessories, Footwear

Notable: Designer Labels for Less
Many designers have introduced bridge collections (second lines) which are less costly but similar in cut and design to their couture lines. The cost is less because they usually use lower priced fabrics and construction occurs out of the country. By "knocking off" themselves these designers have created new opportunities for customers as well as for themselves. Look for the following: DKNY (Donna Karan New York), Anne Klein II, Calvin Klein Sport, Oscar de la Renta Studio, But, Gordon (Gordon Henderson), Perry Ellis Portfolio, and Emanuel (Ungaro).

Tanner Factory Store
Lakeside Marketplace
(See: Outlet Malls)

Tanner is well known for its classic women's sportswear and we were not disappointed. Although the stock seemed somewhat diminished from our first visit, the quality was high. Our favorite - the beautiful cotton knits. They also carry accessories including belts, costume jewelry, and scarfs. Approximately 50% off retail.

Upper Half
3408 N. Southport
Chicago, IL
(312) 477-0494
Fall-Winter M-F 10-9 Sat. 10-8 Sun. 11-6
Summer M closed T-Sat. 3-8 Sun. 11-6

The Upper Half is wonderful! It is an outlet for local knitters' creations as well as imported ones. It is full of hand knit sweaters in natural fibers (children's are acrylic), scarfs, and scatter rugs. The owner is considering importing some Irish knits, but as of now everything is knit on needles rather than on machines. We had a delightful time looking at the gorgeous one-of-a-kind designs, picking out Christmas presents, and just talking to the sales woman who was knitting as we spoke!

Winona Knits
Factory Outlet Centre
(See: Outlet Malls)

Winona Knits sells quality sweaters for men and women from, not surprisingly, the Winona Knitting Mills. The fully independent retail corporation has doubled in size more than four times since it was formed in 1977. We thought an especially nice touch was having the correctly colored turtlenecks to go with the sweaters!

CHILDREN'S APPAREL

Burlington Coat Factory Warehouse
Talisman Center
Golf Rd. & Washington St.
Glenview, IL
(708) 998-3440

Harlem & Foster Aves.
Chicago, IL
(312) 763-6006

Lincoln & Crawford
Matteson, IL
(708) 748-9393

Barrington & Irving Pk.
Hanover Park, IL
(708) 213-7600

So. Cicero & 84th St.
Burbank, IL
(708) 636-8300

Villa Oaks Shop'g Ctr.
Villa Park, IL
(708) 832-4500

Arlington Plaza
Arlington Hts, IL
(708) 577-7878

920 Milwaukee Ave.
Libertyville, IL

Century Consumer Mall
Merrillville, Ind
(219) 736-0636

Hours vary as to location.

Burlington carries children's clothing for ages "Kindergarten to College". Merchandise is current season, first quality and the discount ranges from 25% to 60%. Baby furniture is available.
See Also: Women's and Men's Apparel, Footwear, Linens

Carter's Factory Outlet
Factory Outlet Centre
(See: Outlet Malls)
(414) 857-2049

Lighthouse Place
(See: Outlet Malls)

Carter's Factory Outlet at the Factory Outlet Centre is large and, when I visited, was relatively busy. The selection was good in all areas - infant, toddler and children's apparel. Some tags had just the Carter price and others had a comparable value listed. There were several racks with signs stating an additional 25% would be taken off at the register.

They were also running a special sale where by buying $50 of merchandise you could get an additional $10 off. The amount off increased as the amount purchased increased. Obviously a good place to try if you have small children!

Children's Outlet
The Annex
175 W. Golf Road
Schaumburg, IL 60195
(708) 884-6170
M-F 10-9   Sat. 10-6   Sun .11-5

The Children's Outlet is associated with The Children's Place which is now privately owned. The latter is developing an outlet strategy which is partially defined by location and clientele. This location receives merchandise which has been marked down elsewhere, then they discount further with "red tag sales", etc. They carry boys' and girls' apparel, size newborn to 14. Brand names noted include Bugle Boy, Gloria Vanderbilt, Ocean Pacific and their own label, Memento.

Chocolate Soup
602 Green Bay Road
Winnetka, IL
(708) 446-8951
M-Sat. 10-5:30   Th. 10-8   Sun. 12-5

Chocolate Soup is absolutely terrific! We understand why ladies fly to Chicago just to shop here! The store was jam packed mainly with the exclusive Chocolate Soup styles. At this outlet, merchandise is always 40% off the tag price and during sales such as the one we attended, 60% off. My favorite - the appliqued clothes - or perhaps the beautiful $30 Christmas dress. Wonder when the boys will marry, wonder when...

"Just Kids"
4202 West Belmont Ave.
Chicago, IL
(312) 202-0203
M,W 9:30-5:30 Th,F 9:30-9
Sat. 9:30-5:30 Sun. 10:30-5:30

Located next to Sportique Fashion Outlet and just down from Lorraine Lingerie, "Just Kids" Childrenswear Fashion Outlet was having its Grand Opening the day we visited. They carry infant, toddler, and boys and girls sizes up to 16 with a limited selection of newborn. The Okie Dokie, corduroy, flowered skirt and T-shirt caught our eye immediately! It was $14.99 from $22.99. The owner indicated that they both buy direct and through wholesalers thus the labels they carry may vary from time to time. There is convenient parking on the street or in the parking lot on Keeler just north of Belmont Ave. Note that they are closed on Tuesday.

Lord & Taylor Clearance Center
Town & Country Mall
445 E. Palatine (Palatine and Arlington Hts. Rd.)
Arlington Heights IL
(708) 259-4211
M-F 10-9 Sat. 10-6 Sun. 11-5

Lord and Taylor operates three clearance centers around the country, one of them in Arlington Heights in the Town & Country Mall. This center receives past season merchandise from numerous stores in this general section of the country. The items are at least 35% off the last marked down price, and Thursday through Monday there are various racks marked down as much as 60%. The store is organized according to departments. The Young People's Shop consisted of one rack at our last visit but merchandise varies greatly and at another time the selection may be far greater.
See Also: Women's and Men's Apparel, Lingerie

Marshalls
The following store is the largest:

95th & Cicero (294 South, exit 95th St. east)
Oaklawn, IL
(708) 424-8388

Call 1-800-MARSHAL for the store nearest you.

Hours vary as to location.

Marshalls always seems to have a good selection of children's clothes at reasonable prices. It's a good place to shop for clothes for your own children or grandchildren or to locate gifts for others.
See Also: Women's and Men's Apparel, Fashion Accessories, Housewares

Morris & Sons Co.
River West Plaza
555 W. Roosevelt Road
Chicago, IL 60607
(312) 243-5635
M-Sat. 9-5:30 Sun. 9-4

555 W. Roosevelt Road turned out to be a mini shopping center with Morris & Sons Co. located, as they say, at the "top 'o' the Bank". We climbed the stairs, rang the bell, and were buzzed in. The store carries mainly men's and women's apparel, but does have a limited selection of truly gorgeous children's high fashion apparel, mainly girls' clothing size Toddler to 7, and occasionally boys' clothing Toddler to 8 or 9. Be sure to ask how you can get on their mailing list and be notified of their once a year private sale. Although they do not offer alterations, there is a tailor located in a shop across the hall.
See Also: Women's and Men's Apparel

Nike Factory Outlet

Until December 1991	After December 1991
12225 71st Street	Lakeside Marketplace
Kenosha, WI 53142	(See: Outlet Malls)

The Nike Factory Outlet located across Hwy 50 from the Factory Outlet Centre is large and fully packed. They carry a limited selection of infant and toddler sizes up to size 20. Their markdown is approximately 30% to 40% with special sales the week of July 4th and Labor Day.
See Also: Women's and Men's Apparel, Footwear

Oshkosh B'Gosh
Lakeside Marketplace
(See: Outlet Malls)
(414) 857-9224

Oshkosh B'Gosh The Genuine Article carries some women's, some men's, and mostly children's apparel - toddlers, girls 4-6x, boys 4-7. They also carry a number of accessories including socks, hats, purses, and diaper bags. The regular retail price was not marked, but I was told that discounts range from 20% to 50%. Sale items were marked with a red sticker and an additional percentage was taken off at the register. The boys size 4-7 bibs with florescent trim were $20. The store is spacious and well laid out.

Otiswear
1971 N. Halsted
Chicago, IL
(312) 943-5151
M-W 11-7 Th 11-8 F 11-6 Sat. 10-6 Sun. 12-5

Otiswear is a manufacturer's outlet featuring 100% cotton knitwear for women and children (mostly for girls, but termed unisex). The cotton is double ply and has a wonderful feel. Attractive styles. Ask about laundering.
See Also: Women's and Men's Apparel

Polo - Ralph Lauren
Lighthouse Place
(See: Outlet Malls)
(219) 874-9442

I am always excited about seeing and shopping the Polo-Ralph Lauren outlet at Lighthouse Place and apparently everyone else is too as the store always seems quite busy, especially during seasonal sales. It carries a limited selection of boys' and girls' apparel from size 4 to 20. Read the tags as they will tell you whether the item is first quality or irregular. Unfortunately they no longer take phone orders because of competition with their regular retail stores, but phoning first will help you to determine whether or not the children's apparel selection includes what you need. The sales clerks are friendly, patient, and very helpful.
See Also: Women's and Men's Apparel, Footwear, Linens

Spiegel Outlet Stores

1105 W. 35th St.	9950 Joliet Rd.
Chicago, IL	Countryside, IL
220 S. Waukegan Rd.	1432 Butterfield Rd.
Deerfield, IL	Downers Grove, IL
540 S. Route 59	4 Orland Park Pl.
Naperville, IL	Orland Park, IL
1331 N. Rand Rd.	200 E. North Ave.
Palatine, IL	Villa Park, IL
Gurnee Mills	Hours vary as to location.
(See: Outlet Malls)	

The Spiegel Outlet Stores have everything including children's apparel. The selection is somewhat limited-mainly sportswear (T-shirts and jeans at our last visit), but sizes range from Infant on up. We noted that boys' grey Dockers, size 8, ran $14.99 from $26.00. The atmosphere is as pleasant as the prices with attractive displays, soft music, and ample space to move around.

See Also: Women's and Men's Apparel, Lingerie, Fashion Accessories, Footwear, Furniture, Housewares, Linens

Sportmart

Schaumburg
1015 E. Golf Rd
Schaumburg, IL
(708) 517-7701

River North
440 N. Orleans St
Chicago, IL
(312) 222-0900

Lakeview
3100 N. Clark Street
Chicago, IL
(312) 871-8501

Bricktown
6420 Fullerton Ave.
Chicago, IL
(312) 804-0044

Rt. 59 & E. New York Ave.
Fox Valley, IL
(708) 851-8890

1500 S. Harlem Ave.
North Riverside, IL
(708) 366-6600

1385 Orland Park Place
Orland Park, IL
(708) 460-0900

9633 S. Cicero Ave
Oak Lawn, IL
(708) 636-0501

1500 S. Torrence Ave.
Calumet City, IL
(708) 895-0901

255 Roosevelt Road
Lombard, IL
(708) 620-0901

240 E. Dundee Road
Wheeling,IL
(708) 520-4321

7233 W. Dempster St
Niles, IL
(708) 967-7601

Hours vary as to location.

Sportmart is a discount chain with numerous stores in the Chicago area. They carry all manner of sports apparel including children's. Boys' sizes range from 4 to 20 while girls' range from 4 to 14.

They also carry NFL official licensed products, sports' equipment, and athletic shoes.
See Also: Women's and Men's Apparel, Footwear

T. J. Maxx
There are numerous locations.
The following are two of the largest:

135 Skokie Hwy   7250 Dempster
Highland Park, IL   Morton Grove, IL
(708) 831-1500   (708) 966-4483

Hours vary as to location.

T. J. Maxx has a good selection of children's name brand clothes at reasonable prices. Maybe that's why we always see lots of children both in and out of carts!
See Also: Women's and Men's Apparel, Fashion Accessories, Footwear

Upper Half
3408 N. Southport
Chicago, IL
(312) 477-0494
Fall-Winter M-F 10-9 Sat. 10-8 Sun .11-6
Summer M closed T-Sat. 3-8 Sun .11-6

The Upper Half is wonderful! It is an outlet for local knitters' creations as well as imported ones. It is full of hand knit sweaters in natural fibers (children's' are acrylic), scarfs, and scatter rugs. The owner is considering importing some Irish knits, but as of now everything is knit on needles rather than on machines. We had a delightful time looking at the gorgeous one of a kind designs, picking out Christmas presents, and just talking to the sales woman who was knitting as we spoke!
See Also: Women's and Men's Apparel

LINGERIE

Barbizon
Factory Outlet Centre
(See: Outlet Malls)

The lingerie at Barbizon starts at 40% off the regular price. There are also special seasonal clearances. We found first quality merchandise at really good prices - a half slip for $3.00, full length for $6.00, a $44.00 robe for $13.00, a $33.00 night gown for $9.00. Making it really easy to shop were the colored rings on the hangers to denote size and the extremely pleasant and helpful clerks. No wonder this store won "Store of the month" so many times in 1990!

Carol Hochman Lingerie
Factory Outlet Centre   Lighthouse Place
(See: Outlet Malls)   (See: Outlet Malls)

Carole Hochman manufactures beautiful lingerie under the following labels: Christian Dior, Carole Hochman, Sara Beth and Lily of France. While there was approximately 35% off the regular price on the front racks, for instance a Dior nightgown was marked from $80 to $52, there was an irregular rack at the back of the store with dots marking the problem area with a higher percentage of savings. A nightgown on this rack, which I thought was repairable, was $60 marked to $23.99. Besides the beautiful merchandise, special mention should also be made of the attractive dressing rooms!

Gilligan O'Malley
Lakeside Marketplace
(See: Outlet Malls)

Although there are labels other than Gilligan O'Malley, be assured that all merchandise here in the outlet store is sewn by Gilligan, and if the quality is not first, it is marked irregular on the ticket (a common practice). In fact there was a special rack of summer irregulars for 50% off the marked price (the regular retail price was not shown). On a regular rack nearby a brightly colored terry shower or pool cover-up caught our eye. Suggested retail was $55.00, outlet priced at $36.97.

Hensen Lingerie Factory Store
Lakeside Marketplace
(See: Outlet Malls)

I was thrilled when I found this outlet in the Lakeside Marketplace as I like Hensen, but consider them costly. While I stocked up on my regular style in colors I hadn't even seen, at almost 50% off, Nancy W. headed for the special sale rack. We discovered they don't accept out of town checks, but we still left happy.

L'eggs Hanes Bali
Factory Outlet Centre
(See: Outlet Malls)

Besides a good selection of hosiery, there is also a variety of Bali lingerie in this outlet. The sales staff is friendly and helpful.
See Also: Fashion Accessories

Lord & Taylor Clearance Center
Town & Country Mall
445 E. Palatine (Palatine and Arlington Hts. Rd.)
Arlington Heights, IL
(708) 259-4211
M-F 10-9   Sat 10-6   Sun 11-5

Lord and Taylor operates three clearance centers around the country, one of them in Arlington Heights in the Town & Country Mall. This center receives past season merchandise from numerous

stores in this general section of the country. The clothes are at a minimum 35% off the last marked down price, and Thursday through Monday there are various racks marked down as much as 60%. The lingerie is usually located in the back to the left although we've also found it in the back on the right. Merchandise varies considerably depending on the time of year but we've always found a good selection of lingerie from which to choose. Luckily there are dressing rooms and rest rooms!
See Also: Women's and Men's Apparel, Children's Apparel, Fashion Accessories

Lorraine Lingerie & Lounge Wear
4220 W. Belmont Ave.
Chicago, IL
(312) 283-3000
M-F 9-4   Sat. 9-5   Closed Sunday

Lorraine's is a factory outlet - made in the USA! It's a no frills, warehouse type atmosphere with a security guard at the door and racks upon racks of women's gowns, robes, slips, PJs, etc. There is a full range of sizes (large sizes to 3X) and the racks are refilled with new selections everyday. We especially liked a pajama set, navy with flowers on top and coordinated bottoms with navy and white stripes. It was priced at $31.20 from $52.00 and was probably one of the most expensive items. A nice touch was the availability of gift boxes for your purchases - limit two. The one draw back was the lack of a dressing room.

Maidenform
Lakeside Marketplace   Lighthouse Place
(See: Outlet Malls)   (See: Outlet Malls)

Besides the Maidenform label, the store also carries Oscar de la Renta underwear and Dreamtime sleep wear. Displayed near the front door was our favorite, an Oscar de la Renta camisole top, regularly priced at $40.00, outlet priced at $26.00 with tap pants to match, $36.00 for $23.50. The store carries first quality discontinued and closeout merchandise. Watch for the clearance and exceptional value racks and enjoy the good selection!

Spiegel Outlet Stores

1105 W. 35th St.	9950 Joliet Rd
Chicago, IL	Countryside, IL
220 S. Waukegan Rd.	1432 Butterfield Rd
Deerfield, IL	Downers Grove, IL
540 S. Route 59	4 Orland Park Pl.
Naperville, IL	Orland Park, IL
1331 N. Rand Rd.	200 E. North Ave.
Palatine, IL	Villa Park, IL

Gurnee Mills
(See: Outlet Malls)

Hours vary as to location.

The Spiegel Outlet Stores have what seems like everything including lingerie and there are several of these outlets in the Chicago area. During one visit I was able to purchase an Adrienne Vittadini flannel gown for a very modest sum and it continues to be one of my favorite lounge outfits! Throughout the store the atmosphere is as pleasant as the prices with attractive displays, soft music, and ample space to move around.
See Also: Women's and Men's Apparel, Children's Apparel, Fashion Accessories, Footwear, Furniture, Housewares, Linens

RESALE

B. J.'s Designer Resale & Consignment Boutique
9 E. Superior
Chicago, IL 60611
(312) 642-8303
M-F 11-7   Sat. 11-6   Closed Sunday

B.J. Ashley, who owns B. J.'s, advertises that she brings "Beverly Hills Clothes from the rich and famous to Chicago". (We thought that everyone who was rich and famous already lived in Chicago!!) The labels we saw included Oscar de la Renta, YSL, Beene and Armani. The merchandise ranges from shoes, bags, and jewelry to sports and eveningwear. This is a great place to recycle - either buying or selling!

Entre-Nous Designer Resale Shop
21 E. Delaware Pl
Chicago, IL 60611
(312) 337-2919
M-F 11-6   Sat. 11-5

Entre-Nous is a designer resale shop that prices merchandise at approximately 10% of cost! While the shop is small, it is jam packed with goodies - everything from jewelry and handbags, to suits, sportswear, eveningwear and furs. All your favorite labels at incredible prices if you're in to used but nice or a great place to consign your items if you're into selling. We sometimes are and this is one of the best places we've seen!

Rag Trade
67 East Oak
Chicago, IL
(312) 280-0074
M-F 11:30-5:30   Sat. 11:30-5   Sun. closed

The Rag Trade, formerly known as **The Fashion Exchange**, advertises itself as carrying resale, vintage, and pastiche clothing. At the time of our visit, we found the selection of menswear to be better than that of the women's, and both to be mainly resale. We took note of the men's Burberry raincoat with lining for $100.00 and the men's suede jacket from Saks for $60.00. They also had handbags, jewelry and shoes. The space is very limited and was packed full, both with merchandise and customers. Call for an appointment if you're interested in consignment.

Second Child
954 W. Armitage Ave.
Chicago, IL
(312) 883-0880
M-Sat. 10-6   Sun. 12-5

Christie Davis and Amy Helgren operate a terrific children's resale shop in Lincoln Park called The Second Child. This is really upscale resale with limited but well organized space. They carry up to size 14 but when we visited smaller sizes prevailed. There are color coded tickets to indicate the percentage off the marked price if a garment has been there more than two months. After two months the item is marked down 20%, after three 50%. Besides kid's clothes, there were also some maternity clothes, toys, and various accessories such as the Graco Stroller we noticed for $50.00. There are two major sales - one in January and one in July. Get on the mailing list for advance notice. If you're interested in selling clothes, they'd like you to call first and set up an appointment. They are very selective in their choice of merchandise and pay the consignee 40% of the selling price.

Most, if not all, of the apparel shops carry some fashion accessories. The apparel shops that made it into this section, however, are those with accessories so good they merit special attention.

FASHION ACCESSORIES

American Tourister

Lakeside Marketplace   Lighthouse Place
(See: Outlet Malls)   (See: Outlet Malls)

Gurnee Mills
(See: Outlet Malls)

If you like American Tourister, need luggage, and want to save some money - this is it. They carry luggage, briefcases and travel products at 40% to 70% off and will ship anywhere in the U.S. For the best bargains look at their seconds. At their Birch Run store in Michigan, Nancy B. and I found a hanging bag, two medium bags and a tote bag for $100.00.

Anko Also

Lakeside Marketplace   Lighthouse Place
(See: Outlet Malls)   (See: Outlet Malls)

Besides the lovely knits, this outlet is especially outstanding for its selection of costume jewelry. The jewelry is arranged according to color (a marvelous array of color)! Besides being perfect for their type of garment, unique pieces can be found for any outfit.
See Also: Women's and Men's apparel

Anne Klein Outlet

Lakeside Marketplace   Lighthouse Place
(See: Outlet Malls)   (See: Outlet Malls)
(414) 857-9495

Anne Klein carries a good selection of her accessories including jewelry (necklaces, earrings, pins), watches, belts, and handbags. In general we found the merchandise superb, the saleswomen friendly and helpful, and the bargains galore! A

black dial, round faced, gold bracelet watch we'd admired at Marshall Fields for $150 was priced at $100 here. As in most of the Lakeside outlets there was a mailing list sign up sheet - we signed !
See Also: Women's and Men's Apparel

Bally Outlet Store
Gurnee Mills Mall
(See: Outlet Malls)

Bally Outlet Store is fabulous! Besides the famous Bally shoes for men and women, the outlet also carries handbags, attache cases, luggage, small leather accessories, ties, and a few leather jackets. No matter what the item, the leather is superb! Bally is located in the S-shaped Gurnee Mills Mall in the bottom line of the S, number 743.
See Also: Footwear

Casual Corner Clearance Center
Town & Country Mall
445 E. Palatine (Palatine & Arlington Heights Rd)
Arlington Heights, IL
(708) 577-5333
M-F 10-9 Sat. 10-6 Sun. 11-5

This clearance center carries a large selection of costume jewelry. It's definitely worth checking here for the latest look. They also have a limited selection of watches.
See Also: Women's and Men's Apparel

Cosmetic Center
Loehmann's Plaza   Yorkshire Plaza
240 East Golf Road   4348 E. New York St.
Arlington Heights, IL   Aurora, IL
(708) 364-0200   (708)820-8090

Springbrook Shop. Ctr
142 E. Lake St.
Bloomingdale, IL
(708)893-2500

Ridge Plaza
940 W. Dundee Rd.
Buffalo Grove, IL
(708)259-6700

Chestnut Court
7511 Lemont Rd.
Darien, IL
(708)910-4000

Mainstreet Square
2948 Finley Rd.
Downer's Grove, IL
(708)953-2100

Holiday Plaza
4747 N. Harlem
Harwood Heights, IL
(708)775-0080

Crossroads
139 Skokie Valley
Highland Park, IL
(708)831-1090

Clark & Diversey
2817 N. Broadway
Lincoln Park, IL
(708)935-2600

Highland Square
797 Golf Rd.
Morton Grove, IL
(708)965-8800

15240 S. Grange Rd.
Orland Park, IL
(708)403-7440

Hours vary as to location.

There are several Cosmetic Centers in the Chicago area, hopefully you can find one that's convenient. While they advertise 10% to 50% off, most items we noted were only discounted the 10% - yet 10% is 10%. They didn't have the face mask by Elizabeth Arden that I wanted and they didn't carry the brand lipstick I use, but they seemed to have everything else! Their inventory depends on overstocks in the department stores so it does fluctuate - keep checking and shop their sales.

E. J. Plum
Lakeside Marketplace
(See: Outlet Malls)

E.J. Plum has socks galore. We found a variety of labels besides the Plum label including Members Only, Camp and Christian Dior.

Filene's Basement
State and Madison
Chicago, IL

Gurnee Mills
(See: Outlet Malls)

One Schaumburg Place
Schaumburg, IL

Hours vary as to location.

Filene's Basement, the original off-price bargain basement, has arrived in the Chicago area! Headquartered in Boston, the basement of Filene's is famous throughout the Northeast for its specially priced merchandise which comes from manufacturers' and designers' overruns or canceled orders and buyouts from major stores - including jewelry stores. The jewelry department is a must visit when "doing" Filene's. In this section we also found an array of scarfs, belts, and hosiery.
See Also: Women's and Men's Apparel, Fantastic Sales

Great Lakes Jewelry
104 E. Oak St.
Chicago, IL 60611
(312) 266-2211
M-Sat. 10:30-5:30

Forget Michigan Avenue! Take note of Oak Street, and if you're in the market for sterling silver jewelry head straight for 104 E. Oak St. and Great Lakes Jewelry (down the stairs and in the door to the right). They manufacture a lot of the sterling jewelry that they carry and it's all 50% off! Nancy purchased a gorgeous bracelet for $50 that she'd seen elsewhere for $100. While we happen to think their forte is high fashion, contemporary sterling, they also carry ivory, 14K gold, some estate pieces, and offer repair service. (They repaired a sterling silver candelabra for me for a modest sum and did an excellent job.)

L'eggs Hanes Bali
Factory Outlet Centre
(See: Outlet Malls)

Although we saw a lot of "slightly imperfect" tags in this outlet, we decided to try it and see. After wearing two of the three light support Hanes pantyhose that I purchased for $10.71, I can say I'm pleased. I didn't notice the imperfection, whatever it was, and the price was right! Besides a good selection of hosiery, there was also a variety of lingerie.
See Also: Lingerie

Leather Manor
Lakeside Marketplace   Lighthouse Place
(See: Outlet Malls)   (See: Outlet Malls)
(414) 857-9494

The Leather Manor carries all types of leather goods including handbags, luggage, briefcases, jackets, and designer accessories. Designer names include Carlo Amboldi, Valentino Orlandi, and Marco Avane. They also carry replicas of Coach and Dooney and Bourke. We were told their discount starts at 50% off retail with quarterly sales and periodic unannounced sales. The final sale items are at the back of the store. A Carlo Amboldi navy and gray handbag on the back wall was marked from $56 to $34.99 to the final sale price of $27.99.

Liz Claiborne Outlet Store
Lakeside Marketplace
(See: Outlet Malls)

The Liz Claiborne Outlet Store carries a good selection of accessories including scarfs, hosiery, sun glasses, and occasionally soft sided luggage, as

well as jewelry and a vast array of handbags. These items are discontinued, leftovers, odd lots or overruns and are located along the right side as you enter. There's also a small selection of men's furnishings on the left at the front of the men's section.
See Also: Women's and Men's Apparel

Loehmann's

Village Plaza	Loehmann's Plaza
Dempster & Harlem	320 East Golf Rd
Morton Grove, IL	Arlington Hgts, IL
(708) 966-1350	(708) 228-5570
Finley Square Mall	Matteson Town Center
Downers Grove, IL	Matteson, IL

Hours vary as to location.

Loehmann's is one of the original designer off-price stores and is definitely one of our favorites for women's accessories as well as apparel. They have wonderful scarfs, handbags, belts, hats, and a limited selection of giftware. Select your purchases carefully as merchandise can only be exchanged; they just recently began accepting charge cards. In the Chicago area the largest store with the best selection is in Morton Grove.
See Also: Women's and Men's Apparel

Notable: Jewelers Row
The area may look nondescript but to "those who know" the upper floors of buildings at 55 E. Washington St., 29 E. Madison St., 5 N. Wabash Ave., and 5 S. Wabash Ave. are where the wholesale jewelry action is and has been for over a century. Price breaks are possible at some locations for bargain hunters as well as retail store representatives.

Lord & Taylor Clearance Center
Town & Country Mall
445 E. Palatine (Palatine and Arlington Hts. Rd.)
Arlington Heights, IL
(708) 259-4211
M-F 10-9 Sat 10-6 Sun 11-5

Lord and Taylor operates three clearance centers around the country, one of them in Arlington Hts. in the Town & Country Mall. This center receives past season merchandise from numerous stores in this general section of the country. The items are at least 35% off the last marked down price, and Thursday through Monday there are various racks marked down as much as 60%. The store carries a varying selection of accessories such as handbags, belts, hats, gloves, and small leather goods.
See Also: Women's and Men's Apparel, Children's Apparel, Lingerie

Lori's Designer Shoes and Accessories
808 W. Armitage Ave. (near Halsted)
Chicago, IL 60614
(312) 281-5655
M-TH 11-7 F,Sat. 11-6 Sun. 12-6

This upscale outlet is a converted house with a sign that is more artful than legible and you definitely don't want to miss what's inside! (We parked on a nearby side street and felt lucky that at least on this trip we had no trouble finding a spot.) The selection was fantastic, the styles current, and although the space was jammed, the merchandise was organized effectively. Besides footwear, the store carries beautiful handbags by top designers, an interesting and varied collection of jewelry, and an impressive display of hosiery. Merchandise starts at 20% off and is marked down from there. Sales in January and July mean 50% off the original price of selected pieces.
See Also: Footwear

Mark   Shale   Outlet
2593 North Elston
(north from Fullerton, in a small mall with Cub Food,
    large parking lot)
Chicago, IL 60647
(312) 772-9600

M-F 10-8   Sat. 10-6   Sun. 12-5

As of our visit this was Mark Shale's only outlet. Ten of their retail stores ship end-of-season remainders, overstocks and other odds and ends here and they're marked from 30% to 70% below original retail. The selection of accessories is limited, but the quality outstanding. The largest variety appears to be in scarfs and belts. There are a few handbags, and some men's shoes.   Definitely take time to look in the display case of giftware located close to the men's section.
See Also: Women's and Men's Apparel

Marshall Pierce & Co.
29 E. Madison St.
Chicago, IL 60602
(312) 372-2415
M-F 9-5   Closed Sat. & Sun.

Go into the building at 29 E. Madison St. and take the elevator to the 9th floor. Go to the door of Marshall Pierce & Co. and the friendly sales staff will buzz you in.   While some of the "upstairs" jewelers on Chicago's famed Jewelers Row do not sell or discount to the public, Marshall Pierce & Co. does. Choose diamond, gemstone, or gold pieces from the display case (at approximately one half the marked price), or order custom pieces. A smooth, 5/16th inch wide, hollow, 14K gold bracelet was $200. They also carry Swiss watches, and some silver pieces. Fine jewelry since 1928.

Marshalls
The following store is the largest:
95th & Cicero (294 South, exit 95th St. east)
Oaklawn, IL
(708) 424-8388

Call 1-800-MARSHAL for the one nearest you.
Hours vary as to location.

    Marshalls has a good selection of jewelry, scarfs, belts and handbags. A yellow patent belt I purchased here on sale for $5.00 "makes" this year's favorite, summer outfit.
See Also: Women's and Men's Apparel, Children's Apparel

Mitchell Leather Shop
Factory Outlet Centre
(See: Outlet Malls)

    We were truly impressed by the quality of leather handbags in this factory outlet store. They're made in Milwaukee and they're beautiful. They also sell Samsonite luggage, attachès and, believe it or not, leather hides. The navy hide we looked at was $60.00. The handbags in the sale bin were approximately 50% off. This is one excellent place to Buy USA.

Off Center Building
300 W. Grand Ave.
Chicago, IL 60601

    The Off Center Building in River North at 300 W. Grand Ave. houses some interesting outlet stores. **Tiffany Millinery** in Suite 200 manufactures hats and sells some to the general public. Their selection was admittedly low at the time of our visit.
See Also: Women's and Men's Apparel

Socks   Galore
Lighthouse Place
(See: Outlet Malls)

Besides the colorful display of socks, we learned that they're all 100% American Made. Refreshing! Socks Galore discounts 35% to 75% and carries such name brands as Christian Dior, E.J. Plum, Ultra Fresh and Hue. We bought a few!

Notable: Do they Really Sell it All?
No! But it has to go somewhere and the trick is to discover where. Occasionally unsold merchandise is shipped out after two markdowns (to places like the Arlington Hts., IL   Lord and Taylor Clearance Center, or Last Call in Austin, Texas). Sometimes there is a special sale room or floor (check out the 6th floor of the downtown Lazarus next time you're in Columbus, Ohio). Often they "hide" clothes on a sales rack in the back of the store marking items down further and further with little fanfare and only a wisp of a sign (Judith and I were escorted to the back room at Isaacson's in Atlanta and found terrific buys on the unmarked racks). Or they have one whopper of a sale with items drastically reduced for a couple days. We won't even mention the stores that file it in their back rooms and bring it out year after year. Tacky, tacky!

Spiegel Outlet Stores

1105 W. 35th St.	9950 Joliet Rd.
Chicago, IL	Countryside, IL
220 S. Waukegan Rd.	1432 Butterfield Rd.
Deerfield, IL	Downers Grove, IL
540 S. Route 59	4 Orland Park Pl.
Naperville, IL	Orland Park, IL

1331 N. Rand Rd.   200 E. North Ave.
Palatine, IL   Villa Park, IL

Gurnee Mills
(See: Outlet Malls)   Hours vary as to location.

Along with everything else Spiegel Outlet Stores carry a varying array of accessories. One counter houses watches, at a special price during our last visit, as well as perfume and cologne. There were also a few handbags, belts, and scarfs.
See Also: Women's and Men's Apparel, Children's Apparel, Lingerie, Footwear, Furniture, Housewares, Linen

T. H. Mandy
659 W. Diversey Pkwy   1330 Butterfield Rd.
Chicago,IL 60614   Downers Grove, IL
(312) 975-1800   (708) 953-1771

Downer's Grove, IL   Bloomingdale, IL
708) 241-1070   (708) 980-1060

Vernon Hills, IL   Chicago Ridge, IL
(708) 816-6700   (708) 499-4343

225 N. Michigan Avenue
Chicago, IL   Deerfield, IL
(312) 938-4300   (708) 940-8400

Skokie's Fashion Square
Skokie, IL   Meadowstown Mall
(708) 675-6647   (708) 228-7886

Arlington Heights, IL
(708) 632-1050

Hours vary as to location.

The T.H. Mandy store carries a large selection of accessories - costume jewelry, scarfs, etc. that is worth the time to browse through. It's nice to be able to put the whole outfit together at one location! Check here for the latest in wild and wonderful. It was a kaleidoscope of color the last time we visited! See Also: Women's and Men's Apparel

T. J. Maxx
There are numerous locations.
The following are two of the largest:
135 Skokie Hwy   7250 Dempster
Highland Park, IL   Morton Grove, IL
(708) 831-1500   (708) 966-4483

Hours vary as to location.

Accessories include brand name fragrancies, small leather goods and travel accessories as well as the usual handbags, scarfs, belts, and jewelry - occasionally 14K depending on the store.
See Also: Women's and Men's Apparel, Children's Apparel, Footwear

Ulta^3
Rand Rd & Central Rd   Dempster at Waukegan
Mount Prospect. IL   Morton Grove, IL
(708) 253-2955   (708) 966-0550

North Point Shopping Ctr
Arlington Hts & Rand   Roosevelt at Fairfield
Arlington Heights, IL   Lombard, IL
(708) 577-0375   (708) 268-9300

Rte 59 at Aurora Ave
Naperville, IL
(708) 527-0065   Hours vary as to location.

Ulta^3 "The Ultimate Beauty Store" rates a slew of stars. The "3" stands for selection, service, and savings and they succeed in all categories. Their wide variety of merchandise includes cosmetics, fragrances, bath, skin and hair care, professional salon products, hosiery, fashion jewelry, even cards and magazines (10% off). The salon products include Nexus and Paul Mitchel but these particular brands are not discounted. Hosiery includes L'eggs, No Nonsense, and Burlington and runs 40% off. The array of fragrances includes designer labels such as Channel #5 which was priced at $28.79 instead of the usual $35.00. All merchandise is bought directly from the manufacturer. The sales staff rates a special mention as they were not only very helpful, but also very informed. Be sure to check your sales slip as it includes a savings calculation so you know exactly what you've saved!

Wabash Jewelers Mall
21 N. Wabash
Chicago, IL 60602
(312) 263-1757

Built by M. Y. Finkelman and located at 21 N. Wabash on Jewelers Row (which runs along Wabash Avenue from Washington Street to Madison Street), Wabash Jewelers Mall is an indoor mall composed of sixty booths each a company selling jewelry (diamonds, gemstones, 14K gold, sterling silver, etc.) at discount prices - typically 50% off retail. Many booths also offer custom designing and some offer discounts on designer costume jewelry, for example 20% off Carolee and Christian Dior at Ann Krizia Jewelry. Some booths also exhibit estate jewelry, antiques (on one occasion I saw a beautiful silver coffee service), and watches. The various companies sign contracts with Finkelman Co. and agree to a code of ethics - read the informational signs on the walls. This is a truly interesting place to browse as well as to buy.

FOOTWEAR

Bally Outlet Store
Gurnee Mills Mall
(See: Outlet Malls)

Bally Outlet Store is fabulous! Look here for beautiful traditional styles in superb leather that are wonderfully comfortable. They carry footwear and accessories for both men and women. Bally is located in the S-shaped Gurnee Mills Mall in the bottom line of the S, number 743.
See Also: Fashion Accessories

Banister Shoe
Factory Outlet Centre   Lighthouse Place
(See: Outlet Malls)   (See: Outlet Malls)

Gurnee Mills
(See: Outlet Malls)

Banister ("The 40 Brand Shoe Outlet") carries women's and men's name brand shoes including Joyce, Liz Claiborne, Reebock, Capezio, and Pappagallo. I was able to purchase a pair of Bandolino black patent pumps originally priced at $70.00, outlet priced at $42.00, for $34.00 on sale.

Brands Fashion Factory Outlets
Lakeside Marketplace   Lighthouse Place
(See: Outlet Malls)   (See: Outlet Malls)

Brands is a collection of 31 select vendors (factory outlets) under one roof. Besides women's and men's apparel there's also a good selection of men's and women's Sebago shoes located towards the back. This store is a fairly recent addition to Lakeside. The "mother store" is located in Lighthouse Place in Michigan City.
See Also: Women's and Men's Apparel

Burlington Coat Factory Warehouse

Golf Rd. & Washington St.
Glenview, IL
(708) 998-3440

Harlem & Foster Aves.
Chicago, IL
(312) 763-6006

Lincoln & Crawford
Matteson, IL
(708) 748-9393

Barrington & Irving Pk.
Hanover Park, IL
(708) 213-7600

So. Cicero & 84th St.
Burbank, IL
(708) 636-8300

Villa Oaks Shop'g Ctr.
Villa Park, IL
(708) 832-4500

Arlington Plaza
Arlington Hts, IL
(708) 577-7878

920 Milwaukee Ave.
Libertyville, IL

Century Consumer Mall
Merrillville, Ind
(219) 736-0636

Hours vary as to location.

Burlington's Footwear department is separately owned, so pay for the shoes before leaving the department. You'll recognize the brand names and it's nice having everything under one roof!
See Also: Women's and Men's Apparel, Children's Apparel, Linens

Capezio Shoes

Lakeside Marketplace
(See: Outlet Malls)

Lighthouse Place
(See: Outlet Malls)

Gurnee Mills
(See: Outlet Malls)

We found a wide variety of familiar brand name labels at Capezio including Pappagallo, Evan Picone, Calvin Klein Sport and Bandolino. While the women's size 5's were limited in number, which didn't please Nancy, there was a large selection in other sizes.

Chernin's Shoes

606 W. Roosevelt Road   Dempster at Waukegan Rd
Chicago, IL   Morton Grove, IL
Men's (312) 966-4655   Men's (708) 966-4655
Women's and children's (312) 939-4080

Finley Square Mall
Butterfield at Finley Rd   Lincoln & Crawford Av.
Downers Grove   Matteson, IL
(708) 620-1400   (708) 481-7070

1401 W. Dundee Road   Diversey & Halsted St.
Buffalo Grove, IL   Chicago (Lincoln Park)
(708) 255-3500

Roosevelt Rd. M-S 9-6 Sun 9:30-5
Others M-F 9:30-9 Sat 9:30-6 Sun 11-5

In our opinion Chernin's Shoes, an off-price footwear chain, definitely lives up to its motto of "the finest shoes for less". They claim to have the "largest selection, finest name brands, Personal Service, and Guaranteed Best Prices" and we tend to agree. Just some of the brand names spotted were Bally, Rockport, Bruno Magli, J. Renee, Anne Klein, Stuart Weitzman, Nunn Bush and Timberland. The day we visited the flagship store on Roosevelt, July 15, a sidewalk sale was in progress. Summer shoes were 30% off Chernin's marked price and one-half off the least expensive if three pairs were purchased. I was able to get a camel, medium heel Bally, a red flat Mario Bruni, and a colorful J. Renee flat for $138.00. I later saw the J. Renee shoes in an exclusive Rockford, IL shoe store marked from $67.00 down to $50.25. I had paid $14.00! As we were shopping on Sunday morning during a thunder storm, the store was busy but not hectic. Besides shoes, they also carry handbags, socks and other accessories. The Lincoln Park store is their newest full-service store, the last one having opened in 1985. (Chernin's also owns the self-service **ShoeMart Express** stores.)

Eddie Bauer
Factory Outlet Centre
(See: Outlet Malls)
(414) 857-7061

As their slogan states, this outlet is "Real Eddie Bauer at unreal prices"! They carry firsts and seconds of overstocked and discontinued merchandise which is shipped weekly from their retail and catalog inventory. The savings run 30% to 70%. The store and the selection are large. Some footwear labels we spotted were Rockport, Timberland and Bernardo in men's shoes. The women's selection was limited at the time of our visit and consisted of Eddie Bauer labels. The selection definitely varies and is generally off season.
See Also: Women's and Men's Apparel, Fantastic Sales

Joan & David
Lakeside Marketplace
(See: Outlet Malls)

We were thrilled to see this outlet open at the mall. They carry wonderful but expensive shoes that we'd love to own someday.

Kenneth Cole Shoes
Lakeside Marketplace
(See: Outlet Malls)

If you're looking for a unique pair of shoes, you may find it here! Kenneth Cole carries a good selection of women's and men's fashion footwear, contemporary handbags and some costume jewelry. The shoes run 30% to 50% below retail which means a $60.00 pair of shoes would cost $39.98 unless you hit a sale in which case you could subtract an additional 25%.

Lori's Designer Shoes and Accessories
808 W. Armitage Ave.
(near Halsted)
Chicago, IL 60614
(312) 281-5655

M-TH 11-7 F,S 11-6 Sun. 12-6

Look carefully as you drive down Armitage as this outlet is a converted house with a sign that is more artful than legible and you definitely don't want to miss what's inside! (We parked on a nearby side street and felt lucky that at least on this trip we had no trouble finding a spot.) The selection was fantastic, the styles current, and although the space was jammed, the merchandise was organized effectively. We found brand name and designer shoes such as Nickels, Perry Ellis, Paloma, Joan and Davis too, Claudia Cruti, Pura Lope, Evan-Picone, and Yves Saint Laurent among others. According to the manager, they usually take three markdowns beginning at 20% off. The merchandise moves from the front around to the side, then down a couple stairs to the back. It was in the back, in the lowest mark down racks, that Nancy B. made the buy of the day - a pair of red, calfskin Maserati heels for $20.00 from $98.00. Look for sales in January and July.
See Also: Fashion Accessories

Lucy's Designer Shoes
301 Happ Rd
Northfield, IL
(708) 446-3818

M-Sat. 10-5:30

Lucy's Designer Shoes, a sister store to Lori's, is smaller with a more limited selection of shoes. The sales are still terrific, however, and the sales girls helpful. We miss the accessories and jewelry!

Nike Factory Outlet
Until December 1991   After December 1991
12225 71st Street   Lakeside Marketplace
Kenosha, WI 53142   (See: Outlet Malls)
M-F 9-9   Sat. 9-7   Sun. 10-6

The Nike Factory Outlet located across Hwy 50 from the Factory Outlet Centre is large and fully packed. They offer a wide range of Nike shoes (limited selection of infant and toddler) and clothes. It's well worth the trip, especially for young athletes who are either constantly growing or wearing out shoes. For those of us into walking, we made note of the Nike Air Healthwalker Plus which sold here for $44.95 instead of the suggested retail of $65. Their markdown is approximately 30% to 40% with sales the week of July 4th and Labor Day.
See Also: Women's and Men's Apparel, Children's Apparel

Polo - Ralph Lauren
Lighthouse Place
(See: Outlet Malls)
(219) 874-9442

What an absolute delight to see such an outstanding selection of Ralph Lauren shoes and boots! The styles ranged from his canvas and country collection to his most tailored, impeccable pump, and then on into dressy. The selection was equally as good for men. Even at outlet prices this footwear is costly, but oh what a way to go!
See Also: Women's and Men's Apparel, Children's Apparel, Linens

---

Notable: Art Galleries
If you're interested in art, try a tour of River North wandering through the various galleries and design studios to the left and right of Orleans Street from the river north to Division.

Poseyfisher Inc.
501 N. Wells St.
Chicago, IL 60610
(312) 644-1749
M-F 11-7 Sat 10-6 Closed Sunday

Poseyfisher Inc. has beautiful, designer shoes at discounts of 20% to 75%. It is one Chicago store, however, that is NOT open on Sunday, so we only looked through the windows the first time. After what we saw, it didn't take us long to return! Enzo, Proxy, Alberto Gozzi, Stuart Weitzman, Anne Klein, Peers - need I say more? While the selection is not huge, it is exciting, especially if your weakness is top of the line, designer footwear. Attractively displayed in the window and on stacked boxes on the first floor, were current fall styles, while downstairs were stacks and racks of further marked down sale shoes. They also have 20% off Evan-Picone hosiery. There is a parking lot about a block away with a $5.00 minimum which we found convenient.

Shoe Town
Meadows Mall   T.H. Mandy Fashion Ctr.
Golf & Algonquin   Butterfield & Highland
Schaumburg, IL   Downers Grove, IL
                                (708) 916-0078
M-F 10-9 Sat. 10-6 Sun. 11-5

Shoe Town has long been a favorite shoe source for name brand and designer shoes. It's quick - just check the racks of shoes under your size - and most often it's productive.

Spiegel Outlet Stores
1105 W. 35th St.   9950 Joliet Rd.
Chicago, IL   Countryside, IL

220 S. Waukegan Rd.   1432 Butterfield Rd.
Deerfield, IL   Downers Grove, IL

540 S. Route 59	4 Orland Park Pl.
Naperville, IL	Orland Park, IL
1331 N. Rand Rd.	200 E. North Ave.
Palatine, IL	Villa Park, IL

Gurnee Mills
(See: Outlet Malls)

Hours vary as to location.

The Spiegel Outlet Stores have everything including footwear. In the men's section we noted Zodiac, Jarman, Bass, and Kenneth Cole. A leather soled moccasin was $79.95 from $140. The women's section was equally as good with a variety of styles and brand names.
See Also: Women's and Men's Apparel, Children's Apparel, Lingerie, Fashion Accessories, Furniture, Housewares, Linen

Sportmart

Schaumburg	River North
1015 E. Golf Rd	440 N. Orleans St
Schaumburg, IL	Chicago, IL
(708) 517-7701	(312) 222-0900
Lakeview	Bricktown
3100 N. Clark Street	6420 Fullerton Ave.
Chicago, IL	Chicago, IL
(312) 871-8501	(312) 804-0044
Rt. 59 & E. New York Ave.	1500 S. Harlem Ave.
Fox Valley, IL	North Riverside, IL
(708) 851-8890	(708) 366-6600
1385 Orland Park Place	9633 S. Cicero Ave
Orland Park, IL	Oak Lawn, IL
(708) 460-0900	(708) 636-0501

1500 S. Torrence Ave.	255 Roosevelt Road
Calumet City, IL	Lombard, IL
(708) 895-0901	(708) 620-0901
240 E. Dundee Road	7233 W. Dempster St
Wheeling, IL	Niles, IL
(708) 520-4321	(708) 967-7601

Hours vary as to location.

Sportmart is a discount chain with numerous stores in the Chicago area. They carry all manner of sports apparel and athletic shoes for men, women, and children, and advertise "name brands for less everyday".
See Also: Women's and Men's Apparel, Children's Apparel

T. J. Maxx
There are numerous locations.
The following are two of the largest:

135 Skokie Hwy	7250 Dempster
Highland Park, IL	Morton Grove, IL
(708) 831-1500	(708) 966-4483

Hours vary as to location.

I always check the footwear section here. I've seen Polo, Cole-Haan, and Via Spiga as well as Liz Claiborne, Bandolino and Nickels.
See Also: Women's and Men's Apparel, Children's Apparel, Fashion Accessories

Unisa
Gurnee Mills
(See: Outlet Malls)

Unisa shoes for women can sometimes be spotted at off-price stores, but what a delight to see a whole store full! They've got the latest colors and comfortable styles.

Wolinsky & Levy, Inc.
River West Plaza
555 W. Roosevelt Road
Chicago, IL
(312) 421-8828
M-S 8:30-5:30 Sun 8:30-4:00

Wolinsky and Levy, Inc. is Store No.15 at 555 W. Roosevelt Road. They carry men's shoes including, at the time we visited, Johnson & Murphy, Jarman, and Bostonian. Bob tried on a J&M wing tip loafer for $80.00, list priced at $125. Even though that shoe didn't fit, the salesman persisted through several others but to no avail. A sign stated they had Bally shoes for $80.00 in sizes 11-15.

Notable: Larger Size Women's Shoes
The Unbound Sole is a shoe shop and catalog specializing in women's shoes sizes 10 to 15. Each month the catalog features 15 to 20 new styles from casual to formal. Call toll free 1-800-322-4256 or write and order the catalog: The Unbound Sole, 1515 N. Central Ave., Phoenix, Arizona 85004.

FABRIC, WALLPAPER, & WINDOWS

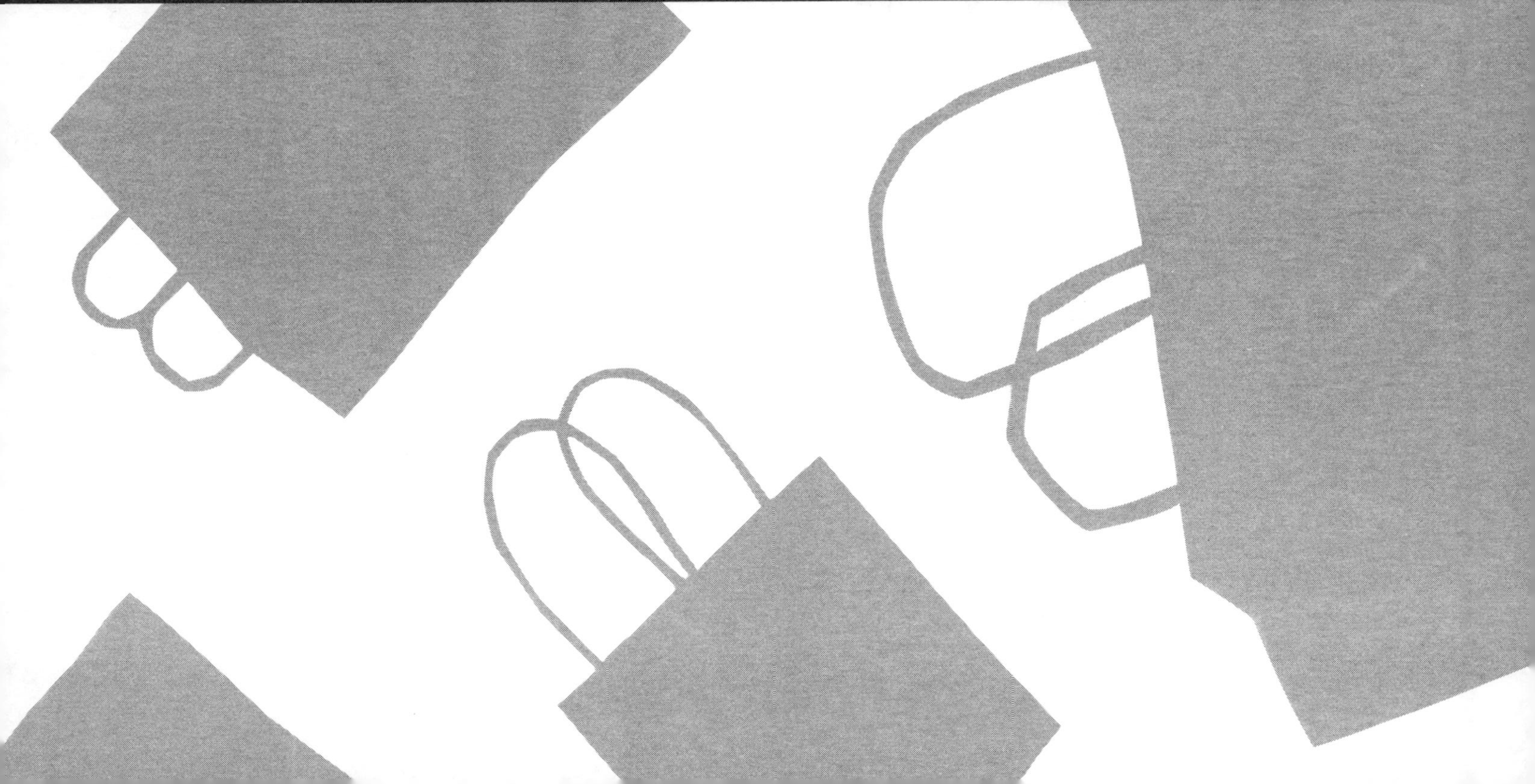

Calico Corners

400 W. Northwest Hwy
(1//2 mile W of Rt. 59)
Barrington, IL.
(708) 304-0080
M 9:30-8:30 T-S 9:30-5:30

896 Waukegan Rd
Lake Forest IL
(708) 234-6800

777 N. York Rd.
(Gateway Square)
Hinsdale, IL.
(708) 920-1955

105 Green Bay Rd.
Wilmette, IL.
(708) 256-1500

Hours vary as to location.

Beautiful fabric. A wide selection of beautiful fabric. In fact the fabric looks so good one must remember to check the tags on each bolt as Calico Corners carries "quality seconds" as well as firsts. Besides the bolts of fabric ready to be cut, including an excellent selection of Waverly, the store also offers samples of "cut to order" fabrics which take about a week to receive. The discount ranges from 30% to as much as 90%. Services available include custom tailoring of bed spreads, drapes, pillows, and upholstery. Nancy again scored the buy of the day when she discovered fabric which matched her new bathroom wallpaper. She plans to sew a pleated border on her quest towels - $7.99 for 1 yard. Check newspapers for special events such as their Home Decorating Idea Showcase during which you can see the latest window treatments, meet representatives from fabric companies, and review the newest collections of decorative fabrics.

Habitat

644 E. Golf Rd.
(1 m.W of Woodfield Mall)
Schaumburg, IL
(708) 882-3200

621 Roosevelt
(Between Highland &
Meyers)
Lombard, IL
(708) 916-8200

610 Route 59   2070 N. Clybourn Ave.
Naperville, IL   Chicago, IL
(708) 355-5100   (312) 404-8500

398 Army Trail Rd.   750 Rand Rd.
(Across from Stratford Sq)(1 mile S. of Rte 22)
Bloomingdale, IL   Lake Zurich, IL
(708) 307-3600   (708) 438-0200

Hours vary as to location.

Habitat with various locations in the Chicagoland area sells name brand wallpaper from 25% to 50% off, blinds up to 75% off, pleated shades and duettes up to 70% off, and Joanna Shutters from 40% to 65% off. They carry Levolor, Bali, DelMar, and Kirsch to name a few. They also have an "off-the-wall" guarantee for wallpaper and an "it's free" guarantee for best price on same product and service. Perhaps the most interesting feature they offer is their Habitat Gallery with hundreds of prints on display and another 1,500 available through catalogs. Frames and color mats are also available. Prices for prints run from $3 to $30 unframed and from $69 on up for framed. Check it out, it may be worth the trip - and they have guides for do-it-yourselfers!

Hart's Fabric Mart
Addison Commons Shopping Center
539 W. Lake St.
Addison, IL
(708) 628-1900
M, Th 10-9 T,W,F 10-6 Sat. 9-5 Sun. 12-5

As we enter the door at Hart's Fabric Mart, what impresses us the most are the numerous, attractive displays - especially of various drapery treatments. Upon closer examination, we also appreciate the tag on each display which states the total cost and then how it breaks down into fabric, and labor, even how much yardage is needed. Their fabric and wallpaper

85

are first quality and run 30% to 70% off. Besides the good selection of in-stock paper (sometimes with fabric to match), they also have books from which you can order. In like manner, they have bolts of fabric in stock as well as hanger samples - featuring as they say, "the best known top design fabric companies in the world... from $5.00 per yd. to $190.00 per yd." Harts custom makes draperies, top treatments, bedspreads, verticals, blinds and shades, and slipcovers, as well as furniture. The whole store impressed us as did the helpful and informative personnel!

Loomcraft

Factory Outlet Centre
(See: Outlet Malls)
(414) 857-2100

Bloomingdale Court
360 W. Army Trail Rd.
Bloomingdale, IL 60108
(708) 351-0511

Deerbrook Mall
126 S. Waukegan Rd.
Deerfield, IL 60015
(708) 205-1611

Grove Shopping Center
13108 W. 75th St.
Downers Grove, IL 60515
(708) 852-1202

3330 N. Clark St.
Chicago, IL 60657
(312) 404-1100

Highpoint Centre
567 E. Roosevelt Rd.
Lombard, IL 60148
(708) 916-8844

Lake View Plaza
15838 LaGrange Rd.
Orland Park, IL 60462
(708) 403-2296

Meadows Town Mall
1400 E. Golf Rd.
Rolling Meadows, IL 60008
(708) 640-8878

University Plaza
1209 Butterfield Rd
Downers Grove, IL
(708) 241-4544

New York Square
4332 Fox Valley Center Dr.
Naperville, IL
(708) 978-0040

Village Crossing Center   5605 Touhy Avenue
6540 W. 95th Street   Skokie/Niles, IL
Oak Lawn, IL   (708) 647-0277
(708) 430-7574

Hours for all of above: M-F 10-9, Sat 10-6, Sun 11-5

645 N. Lakeview Parkway
Vernon Hills, IL
Hours: M 9:30-8:30, Tu-Sat 9:30-5:30, Sun 11-5

Loomcraft is a distributor that buys from various fabric manufacturers. Fabrics included in the selection when we visited were Waverly, American-Textile, and a few by Robert Allen. There are assorted types of fabric, as well as different levels of quality. Read the information on the tags as well as that along the selvage of the fabric itself. You'll find out not only if it's first quality, but also whether or not it's scotch guarded or how it's printed in the first place. Savings are approximately 50% to 70% everyday, with a special clearance section in the back. Sales are final and there is a one yard minimum. There are special custom labor services available if you don't intend to do the sewing yourself.

The recently opened store in Vernon Hills is a warehouse clearance store - note that the hours are different.

> **Notable: An Old Fabric with a New Image**
> Polyester, the fabric we spurned in the 1980s, is making a comeback. Its microfibers are now reputedly finer than silk; eight to nine times finer than the old polyester we remember. While it is soft, drapable, and looks delicate, it can still be washed and doesn't wrinkle. It also breathes and feels wonderful - what more could we want!

Wallpaper Discount Center Factory Outlet
6365 Business Route 20
Belvidere, IL
(815) 544-6001
M-Th 9-7   F-Sat. 9-5

This wallpaper factory outlet has over 90,000 rolls in stock at 33% to 80% off plus special order books from 20% to 33% off retail. The special orders take about a week while the cut to order are ready while you wait. A special discount is available on packaged rolls displayed in the back room. We saw a variety of wallpaper styles attractively displayed with books arranged neatly and organized conveniently according to style.

FURNITURE

Carson Pirie Scott Home Outlet Store
University Plaza
1211-A Butterfield Rd.
(off Frontage Rd. past   Lakehurst (Top Floor)
Homemakers Warehouse) Belvidere Rd. and Route 43
Downers Grove, IL   Waukegan,IL
(708) 810-1090
M-F 10-9   Sat. 10-6   Sun. 11-5

After all the maneuvering to get here, we'd hoped this outlet would be a good one. We were not disappointed. In true warehouse style, stretching ahead of us were rows and rows of upholstered chairs and sofas, to our left were carpet remnants and area rugs, and to our right were electronics. In the area beyond were all the wooden pieces - tables, bedroom and dining room sets, and a wall of curios. They were all discontinued styles and floor samples - some slightly damaged, some with major damage, and all sold "as is". One camel back settee was $347 from $600. An oxblood leather tufted sofa was $767 from $2000. A double beveled glass top table on a brass stand was $312 from $600. Inspect carefully; great bargains abound!

Designer Sample Store
Market Square Shopping Center
2121 N. Clybourn Ave.
Chicago, IL 60614
(312) 871-7732
M-S 10-6   M,Th to 8   Sun 12-5

Formerly known as **Consignment Collection** and now the Designer Sample Store, the owners, Anna Ahlgrim and Char Pieser, are phasing out of consignment pieces and into showroom samples from the Merchandise Mart at 50% to 75% below retail. As you might expect from the Mart, the pieces are upscale and unique. They have an unusually good selection of oriental merchandise, as well as contemporary and traditional. We saw items from Henredon, Baker, Custom Craft, Union National, and Wildwood. The selection varies so check in often. Also offered is a line of custom furniture and upholstery.

As a special treat after shopping, stop in at **Treasure Island**, a grocery store also located in The Market Square. They have wonderful pastries, a special deli, gourmet delights, even a cooking school if you're close enough!

European Furniture Warehouse
2145 W. Grand
Chicago, IL
(312) 243-1955
M,W,F 10-6   Tu., Th., Sat., Sun., 10-5

Advertised as the "Midwest's largest & finest selection of European imports", EFW carries tables, chairs, leather pieces, and a wide selection of marble pieces. (The marble is polyurethane coated and fiberglass backed.)   Everything is imported and 90% is from Italy. Special orders can be made on the leather pieces; for instance, you can upgrade the leather for $100 per grade (1,000 grade is base, then 1500, etc. to 4,000 which is tops). While their pieces include traditional furniture, the greatest selection is in contemporary. Discounts range from 35% to 55%.

Hufford Furniture Co.
310 W. Washington St.
Chicago, IL 60606
(312) 236-4191
M 8:30-7   T-F 8:30-5:30   Sat. 9-1

Hufford Furniture Co. is one of our favorites! They have zeroed in on quality manufacturers of solid oak, cherry and mahogany at savings from 30% to 40% everyday . The store is attractive, well lighted, and everything is beautifully displayed.

There are two main levels, the second handling more moderately priced items. The 6th floor is the clearance center with every item 50% off retail. A sampling of manufacturers includes Bradington Young, Century, Classic Leather, Conover, Ello, Ficks Reed, Henredon, La Barge, Madison Square, Stiffel and Wildwood. There are annual store wide sales which give you an additional 5% off the marked down price. Purchase something or sign the guest list to receive advance notice. Besides knowledgeable, friendly, helpful sales personnel, Hufford, in business since 1899, will refund double the difference if an identical item is found for less at any other store in the state!

Interiors on Consignment
2150 N. Clybourn Ave.
Chicago, IL 60614
(312) 868-0797
Closed Mon., Thurs. 11-8, Sun. 12-5, Other days 10-6
(may vary in summer)

Interiors on Consignment, open only a few months when we visited, had a good selection of what they term "gently used furniture and accessories." At the higher range level was the Century Game Table and four cushioned party chairs for $2950.00 in very good to excellent condition, and the Baker executive type desk, credenza and leather desk chair for $5225.00. Wonderful buys if they suit your purpose. Likewise, this may be the place to check when your student moves into his first apartment. If you're interested in consigning items, there is a one time charge of $10.00 (city) and $15.00 (suburb) which is your only expense. They will come out and evaluate pieces which they price at approximately 2/3 of the original price and then you split 50/50. If the item has not sold in 30 days the price is lowered 50%, then 75%. Just call for an appointment - Ellen and Kenneth V. Kohn, owners.

Mart Sample Store
St. James Crossing
(5 Min.So.of Oakbrook Shopping Ctr.)
818 E. Ogden Ave.
Westmont, IL. 60559
(708) 789-8155

M,TH 10-9 T,W,F 10-6 Sun.11-5

The Mart Sample Store carries designer furniture (showroom floor samples and accessories) from the Chicago Merchandise Mart, as well as some West coast lines not represented at the Mart. They average approximately 40% below retail, although you can get lucky as when Nancy W. purchased an awe inspiring Kinder Harris crystal artwork with the original list price around $1000 for the Mart Sample price of $415. This is definitely the place to try for unique, current, upscale pieces. Dwayne and Sharon Moore, the owners, and their staff are friendly, as well as helpful. They offer interior design service, store delivery, and will ship anywhere in the U.S.
See Also: Fantastic Sales

Phoenix Design
368 W. Huron
Chicago, IL 60610
(312) 951-7945
M,T,Th, F 11-6   Sat. 11-5   Sun. 12-5

Phoenix Design specializes in contemporary furniture. Their ad indicates that they carry The Prairie Collection (F. L. Wright inspired) in Solid Oak, and the "Corbusier Lounger" (in leather $695, in Pony $725). We noted several unique pieces and appreciated the fact that both original and discount prices were listed on the tags.

Spiegel Outlet Stores

1105 W. 35th St.	9950 Joliet Rd.
Chicago, IL	Countryside, IL
220 S. Waukegan Rd.	1432 Butterfield Rd.
Deerfield, IL	Downers Grove, IL
540 S. Route 59	4 Orland Park Pl.
Naperville, IL	Orland Park, IL
1331 N. Rand Rd.	200 E. North Ave.
Palatine, IL	Villa Park, IL
Gurnee Mills	
(See: Outlet Malls)	

Hours vary as to location.

The Spiegel Outlet Stores have everything including furniture. On one of our visits we noticed a desk marked to $59.95 from $129 and a printer table for $49.99 from $99. The sofas, chairs, tables and lamps are displayed effectively in attractive settings.
See Also: Women's and Men's Apparel, Children's Apparel, Lingerie, Fashion Accessories, Footwear, Housewares, Linen

Toms-Price
303 E Front St.
(3 blks. N. of Rt. 38, 3 blks. E of Main St.)
Wheaton, IL
(708) 668-7878
M &Th. 9:30-9 T,W, F, S 9:30-5:30 Sun. 12-5

Toms-Price is my price, my place; I'd like just to move in! What a lovely store, filled with beautiful furniture and accessories, and all at discount prices! The discount runs 25% to 30% off retail with sales adding approximately 5% more. There are summer and winter sales and a special accessories sale in March. THE sale is in November! Among others

they carry Hickory Chair, Henkel-Harris, Jamestown Sterling, Nichols & Stone, Vanguard, Classic Leather and Craftwork Guild. Their commitment is to offer the lowest prices on America's finest furniture. Styles range from Shaker to English Chippendale, and Mission Oak to Country French. Accessories are outstanding, and you could get lost examining the large selection.
See Also: Fantastic Sales

Variations Inc.
3403 N. Ridge Avenue
Arlington Hts., IL
(708) 398-7007
M-F 9:30-5 Sat. 9-2

After weaving around and behind a series of small buildings, we eventually discovered Variations Inc. Not knowing which door to enter, we ended up walking through the manufacturing plant - stopping all work in progress! One begins to understand the 50% savings Variations can offer on its custom laminated furniture and cabinetry - residential or commercial. On display was a multi-section entertainment center for $2400 with rounded corners, brass trim and space for built in speakers, lights, and a section of glass shelves. They can do any look in laminate, and will match wood grain. Fax or bring in a sketch, pictures of what you want, or take advantage of their custom designing. They also work in Corian.

Notable: Learn About Oriental Rugs
To receive the booklet "The Mystique of Oriental Rugs" which includes a variety of interesting information about oriental rugs including how to spot an imposter, write to the Oriental Rug Retailers of America at 1600 Wilson Blvd., Suite 905, Arlington, Va. 22209

Cookware, Dishes, Glassware, Stemware,
Flatware, Utensils and Gadgetry
Plus
China and Crystal, Silver, Vases,
Figurines and Giftware

HOUSEWARES

Bed, Bath & Beyond
Deerbrook Mall on the North Shore
96 S. Waukegan Rd (at Lake-Cook Rd)
Deerfield, IL
(708) 272-6264
M-F 9:30-9   Sat. 9:30-6   Sun. 12-6

1321 East Golf Rd.
(S.W. corner of Golf Rd. and Meacham Rd.)
Schaumburg, IL
(708) 995-0515
M-S 9:30-9   Sun. 10-6

Gurnee Mills
(See: Outlet Malls)

Bed, Bath & Beyond is huge - wear your tennies! They seem to carry everything and lots of it! Besides bath accessories, glassware, cookware, and storage items, we really liked the selection of fine quality mirrors and bath hardware. They advertise 20% to 40% off. Check their ads for specials and sales. See Also: Linens

Brass Factory
Lakeside Marketplace   Gurnee Mills
(See: Outlet Malls)   (See: Outlet Malls)

What's really notable about The Brass Factory besides all the beautiful brass accessories, table bases, and animals, is the brass polish they sell for $5.95. It comes in a tube and, after trying it, both Nancy and I are pleased with the results.

Char Crews, Inc.
670 North Wells   8 Grant Square
Chicago, IL   Hinsdale, IL
(312) 642-2202   (708) 920-0190

Plaza Del Lago
Wilmette, IL
(708) 256-5910

428 Touhy Ave.
Park Ridge,IL
(708) 692-6360

112 Barrington Commons
Barrington, IL
(708) 382-5750

Out of state: call 1-800-323-1972
Hours vary as to location.

Char Crews, Inc. discounts famous name brands of china (Lenox, Royal Doulton, Villeroy & Boch, etc.), crystal, sterling, and stainless (Yamazaki, Oneida, etc.) from 15% to 20%. In the fall and spring, sales subtract another 15% and advance notification is sent to previous purchasers. They do have a Bridal Registry; they do not do engraving or repairing. Except for some of the giftware, the items do not have a price tag, an inconvenience, but the store does have a toll free number. The largest store is in Hinsdale.

Notable: Flea Markets

Interested in one of the better antiques and flea markets in the U.S.? Try the Kane County Flea Market at the Kane County Fairgrounds, St. Charles, IL, (708) 377-2252. It's open the first weekend of every month year-round. Wear boots or old shoes if rainy or wet.

Next, for real down-and-out flea bargaining, try the giant Swap-O-Rama in one of five locations in the Chicago area: Alsip, Melrose Park, Cicero, Monee and Brighton Park.   The biggest is a 670-stall, indoor-outdoor facility in Alsip. It's just off the Tri-State at 129th Street. It's open at 7AM on weekends and on Wednesday. Nominal admission fee.

Crate & Barrel Outlet Store
800 W. North Avenue
Chicago, IL 60622
(312) 787-4775
M-F 10-7   Sat 10-6   Sun 11-5
(Varies according to season)

The Crate & Barrel Outlet Store is absolutely terrific! The location has been changed from N. Wells to 800 W. North Avenue. This location is convenient with limited free parking in the newly constructed strip mall, and the store itself is more spacious. The wonderful, old wooden floors are now cement, but the music and displays remain. There is a wide range of typical C&B merchandise including glassware, pottery, utensils, some furniture, and a great selection of Marimekko fabric. (Children's play furniture was 40% off at the time of our visit.) Naturally the exact merchandise changes and you can find 1st quality items, discontinued items, end-of-season specials, seconds, and occasionally special purchases for the outlet (check the price tags - if the item does not have two prices, regular and outlet, it's probably a special purchase). Be sure to check the bargain rack with closeout items. The overall discount ranges from 25% to 75% off. This is definitely one of our favorite places for browsing as well as buying. A great place to pick up gifts!

Notable: Discontinued but Found
Audrey Rickard, founder of China Trade Limited, searches for long-lost china patterns for clients all over the world. She charges by the relative worth of the china in today's market. She has her own inventory of discontinued china as well as contacts with other china dealers, antique collectors, and resalers. To find china call her at China Trade Limited 708-256-7414.

Crystal Works Factory Outlet
Lakeside Marketplace   Lighthouse Place
(See: Outlet Malls)   (See: Outlet Malls)

Besides their own factory label, Nachtimann, Crystal Works also carries a limited selection of Orrefors and Baccarat crystal at 20% off. The Baccarat Harmony Vase regularly $200 was thus priced at $160. The percentage off is greater on other items such as the crystal wine glass Nancy W. purchased for $6.95 and later saw in a "top drawer" Tulsa furniture store on sale for $22.00. There are also special sales including the "item of the month", Christmas in July, and the ever present clearance table. Besides stemware we saw interesting lamps and decorative pieces.

Dansk Factory Outlet
Lighthouse Place
(See: Outlet Malls)
(219) 879-8300

As we entered the Dansk Factory Outlet the upscale, high tech, dramatic cookware in white caught our eye. We saw in a few minutes that it also came in red, black and navy. Terrific! (The large casseroles were 37% off, running $60 from $95) In the Master Series Stainless steel the percentage off ran 23% on less costly items to 33% on costly ones. Besides cookware, they also had a good selection of tableware in a variety of patterns at up to 45% off. Their traditional Dansk stainless flatware ran $20 to $40 for a 5 piece placesetting. Also in evidence was the familiar Dansk wooden bowls and accessories, carried both in the dark and natural wood. I could have spent a lot in this store - next time I'm going without my husband!

> **Notable: Catalogue by Eddie Bauer**
> To obtain a free copy of Eddie Bauer's new Home Collection Catalogue, call 1-800-426-8020.

Edward Don & Co. Outlet Store
2525 N. Elston Ave.
Chicago, IL
(312) 489-7739

Interested in cooking? Restaurant style? The Don Outlet Store has 1,500 items now available to the public including flatware, glasses, paper and disposable goods, cleaning supplies, china, pots and pans, and gadgets. The selection varies as they stock closeouts, special purchases, and overstocks. Corelle white dinner plates were on special, 6 for $4.00, while heavier weight, Rego, white plates sold for $3.39 each. There was a good selection of bar supplies and small appliances. A Kitchen Aid 5 qt. mixer was $289.00, the 4 qt. $199. Parking is available in a lot on the side of the store. Bon Appetit!

Fuller Brush Factory Outlet
Factory Outlet Centre
(See: Outlet Malls)

I was thrilled to see this outlet in the mall and pleased to see the wide selection of household items at the high quality level I had always associated with Fuller Brush. We found mops for $4.29 and lambs wool dusters for $5.96 (small size) and $7.46 (medium size). I purchased the latter for my two college students hoping it would add enough of an element of fun for them to clean once in a while!

Haeger Potteries Inc.
Seven Maiden Lane
(on Van Buren St., 2 blks south of Rt. 72 in Dundee)
Dundee, IL 60018
(708) 426-3441
M-F 8:30-5   Sat. & Sun. 10-5

The Haeger Pottery Factory Outlet complex has many things in store for you. The pottery, displayed in room after room, includes vases of various sizes and shapes, candle sticks, statues, picture frames, lamps, and even columns. All Haeger items are seconds, discontinued, or one-of-a-kind test pieces. While factory direct prices are terrific, they're even 20% to 50% less during the annual tent sale! There are shopping carts available, restrooms, and plenty of parking. When your shopping is complete, take time to tour the factory, have a floral arrangement custom made for your new vase, or tour their museum - take special note of the huge, W. Goebel, Hummel figurine and its history, as well as the World's Tallest Art Pottery Vase by Haeger. As they state, "Haeger...a fourth generation, family-owned American business since 1871"

Marshalls
The following store is the largest:
95th & Cicero (294 South, exit 95th St. east)
Oaklawn, IL
(708) 424-8388
Call 1-800-MARSHAL for the store nearest you.
Hours vary as to location

With over 375 stores nationwide Marshalls is well known. Their housewares section is towards the back and is worth a quick run through. There are usually oriental lamps and vases, brass items, some silver, a good selection of picture frames, and various gift items.
See Also: Women's and Men's Apparel, Children's Apparel, Fashion Accessories

Mikasa
Lakeside Marketplace   35 N. Waukegan Rd.
(See: Outlet Malls)   Deerfield, IL
(414) 857-2003   (708) 940-7885

Mikasa sells quality crystal, china, pottery, flatware, linens, and accessories at 30% to 60% off.

We saw Berkeley Stemware and Barware for $4.99, suggested retail $13. Northern Lights Stemware of assorted sizes was priced at $6.99-$9.99, suggested retail $20-$27.50. There were also bone china picture frames on sale for $7.99-$17.99. They have a separate customer service desk, will special order items, and will ship UPS for a nominal charge.

Pickard Factory Outlet
782 Corona Ave.
Antioch, IL 60002
(708) 395-3800
M-F 8:30-4

Ever wonder who makes the special china services commissioned for Air Force One, Camp David, Blair House, and American Embassies? Wonder no more - it's Pickard, run by three generations of the Pickard family from its founding in 1893 to the present day. Be sure to pick up the Stars and Stripes brochure which shows the collection (favorite recipes included). The outlet, located right next to the factory, sells items that are all slightly imperfect, except for the limited edition plates, for discounts of 40% to 50% off retail. The decorated dinnerware is sold in sets of 20, 24, or 40. Additional pieces may be purchased individually along with the set. The 20 piece set seemed to range in price from $350 to over $700 depending on style. The items in the undecorated dinnerware (there are at least four different styles in plain white) are sold on an individual basis. If you're ready for fine china, you're ready to visit Pickard. Catalogs available - just call or write.

Royal Doulton
Lighthouse Place
(See: Outlet Malls)

The only thing better than Royal Doulton, is Royal Doulton discounted! The outlet store is full of the beautiful china, figurines, and crystal traditionally associated with Royal Doulton. They carry firsts and seconds with the "best buys", of course, on seconds. Look carefully, some irregularities are hardly noticeable. At the time of our second visit, they had a Christmas special on Royal Albert and Royal Doulton Christmas Dinnerware at up to 80% off. A five piece set, regularly $80-$135 was now $24.95 (Second Quality Limited Available). They accept special orders on all Royal Doulton products and will ship anywhere for a minimal fee.

Sassafras
Lakeside Marketplace   Lighthouse Place
(See: Outlet Malls)   (See: Outlet Malls)

Color, Bold Beautiful Color, in all sorts of home accessories. There's dinnerware (the Lindt-Stymeist 20 piece basic set which retails for $207.60, was priced at $172.31) and baskets and terra cotta accessories and perhaps the most interesting - a large selection of scissors with a huge table filled with slips of paper to try out the scissors! Oh, yes - perhaps the most colorful of all - the soft luggage of all shapes and functions!

Spiegel Outlet Stores
1105 W. 35th St.   9950 Joliet Rd.
Chicago, IL   Countryside, IL

220 S. Waukegan Rd.   1432 Butterfield Rd.
Deerfield, IL   Downers Grove, IL

540 S. Route 59   4 Orland Park Pl.
Naperville, IL   Orland Park, IL

1331 N. Rand Rd.   200 E. North Ave.
Palatine, IL   Villa Park, IL

Gurnee Mills
(See: Outlet Malls)

Hours vary as to location.

Spiegel's, known for its vast array of merchandise, also has a selection of various items classified as housewares - accessories such as lamps, silk trees and plants, as well as cookware and various odds and ends. The selection varies from one trip to the next, but the location of these items is generally towards the back. Its worth the walk to check them out!
See Also: Women's and Men's Apparel, Children's Apparel, Lingerie, Fashion Accessories, Footwear, Furniture, Linen

---

Notable: Stop Junk Mail
Known as bulk mail or direct-mail advertising, this unwanted mail clogs your mailbox and the country's landfills. By writing to Direct Marketing Association or Equifax Inc. and providing the name and address appearing on the labels, the unwanted mail can actually be stopped. For a nominal fee Equifax Inc. has a service called Buyer's Market which allows you to fill out an order form thus remaining on some lists while eliminating others.

Mail Preference Service
Direct Marketing Association
11 W 42nd St. P.O.Box 3861
New York, New York 10163

Equifax Option
P.O.Box 740123
Atlanta, GA 30374

Buyer's Market   Call 1-800-289-7658

Tuesday Morning

Finley Sq. Mall
1524 Butterfield
Downers Grove, IL
(708) 620-0445

F&M Bldg.
840 Roselle
Hoffman Estates, IL
(708) 884-8964

The Landings
16801 Torrence Ave
Lansing, IL
(708) 895-9525

Liberty Mill Plaza
904A Milwaukee Ave
Libertyville, IL
(708) 816-3635

Market Meadows Ctr
1241 Naper Blvd
Naperville, IL
(708) 420-0223

Brookside Plaza
Waukegan & IL. Tlwy
Northbrook, IL
(708) 205-9967

Sunrise Plaza
15641 S 94th Ave
Orland Park, IL
(708) 403-3020

4335 W Oakton
Skokie, IL
(708) 674-2468

80th Place Plaza
20 W. 80th Place
(1 block north of U.S. 30)
Merrillville, Ind.
(219) 769-7181

The Annex of Arlington
19 W Rand Rd
Arlington Heights, IL
(708) 670-9497

Summer: May-June   Fall: Aug.-Sept   Holiday: Oct.-
Dec.   Winter: Feb.-Mar.
(Call for exact dates and hours)

*Note: The Tuesday before each official opening the store is open from 3-7PM for "special customers" or "those in the know"! For instance if the opening day is Thursday May 2,1991- then go the preceding Tuesday April 30, anytime between 3 and 7 PM. This is obviously the best time to see and purchase the new inventory.

Tuesday Morning has 1st quality closeout "gifts" at 50% to 80% off regular retail. The "gifts" range from artwork to linens, wicker, china, glassware,

flowers, brass, ceramics, etc. The quantities are limited and the merchandise varies with each new opening. They are open only four times during the year for a month or two at a time so it's best to be early for best selection! (No, it's not just on Tuesdays!) If you find something you want or need, the savings are fantastic. For instance, we saw Towle Full Lead Crystal goblets, retail $10.00, priced at $1.99. It's also nice to know that they advertise, "Satisfaction Guaranteed Or Your Money Cheerfully Refunded."
See Also: Linens

Waccamaw Pottery

Meadows Town Mall
1400 E Golf Rd
Rolling Meadows, IL
(708) 806-6105

Village Crossing
5545 Touhy Ave.
Skokie, IL 60077
(708) 675-3595

Gurnee Mills
(See: Outlet Malls)
(708) 855-0480

Naperville (to be announced)

M-F 10-9 Sat. 10-6 Sun. 11-5
(Gurnee Mills 11-6)

Waccamaw Pottery is a huge store which advertises that it "guarantees low prices on large quantities of quality merchandise." Inside is every manner of houseware from pottery and china to small appliances, fancy foods, crystal, greenery, baskets, luggage, wicker, and linens. Among the variety of pottery is an excellent selection of Pfaltzgraff. Signs hanging above certain sections advertise additional markdowns from the marked price - for instance the Plallzgraff boxed dinnerware sets were 20% off when we visited. Likewise, crystal glasses were 33% off. A special attraction in the floral area is their custom flower

108

and craft designs. While you wait, the designer will create an arrangement for you . Also noteworthy is the large selection of oriental accessories including vases, figurines, screens, and some furniture. Be sure to take a basket near the front as you enter the store - you'll need it !
See Also: Linens

BED, BATH, & TABLE LINENS

Bed, Bath & Beyond
Deerbrook Mall on the North Shore
96 S. Waukegan Rd (at Lake-Cook Rd)
Deerfield, IL
(708) 272-6264
M-F 9:30-9 S 9:30-6 Sun 12-6

1321 East Golf Rd. (S.W. corner of Golf and Meacham)
Schaumburg, IL
(708) 995-0515
M-S 9:30-9 Sun. 10-6

Gurnee Mills
(See: Outlet Malls)

Bed, Bath & Beyond is huge - wear your tennies! They seem to carry everything and lots of it! The linens go on and on, row after row. They advertise 20% to 40% off and that held true with the Laura Ashley king size dust ruffle we purchased at $79.99. (The Laura Ashley store at Northbrook - practically around the corner - was putting it on sale the following week for $82.00 or 25% off.) Check their ads for specials and sales.
See Also: Housewares

Burlington Coat Factory Warehouse
Talisman Center
Golf Rd. & Washington   Harlem & Foster Aves.
Glenview, IL   Chicago, IL
(708) 998-3440   (312) 763-6006

Lincoln & Crawford   Barrington & Irving Pk.
Matteson, IL   Hanover Park, IL
(708) 748-9393   (708) 213-7600

So. Cicero & 84th St.   Villa Oaks Shop'g Ctr.
Burbank, IL   Villa Park, IL
(708) 636-8300   (708) 832-4500

Arlington Plaza
Arlington Hts, IL
(708) 577-7878

920 Milwaukee Ave.
Libertyville, IL

Century Consumer Mall
Merrillville, Ind
(219) 736-0636

Hours vary as to location.

Burlington carries a huge selection of brand name linens and bath accessories at 25% to 50% off retail.
See Also: Women's and Men's Apparel, Children's Apparel, Footwear

Linens & Wares
Village Crossing Shop'g Center
5637 Touhy Ave.
Niles, IL

Commons Center
6328 North West Hy
Crystal Lake, IL

Park Place Shopping Center
1365 North Rand Rd.
Palatine, IL
(708) 394-5655

735 West Main St.
Lake Zurich, IL

Brookville Plaza
461 N. Waukegan Rd.
Northbrook, IL

Prospect Crossing
1219 N. Rand Rd.
Arlington Hgts., IL

Merrillville Plaza
1700 East 8th Ave.
Merrillville, IL

Hours vary as to location.

The "wares" of Linen & Wares is interesting and includes dishes (Nikko, Pfaltzgraff), kitchen utensils (we bought the ones with the big fat, soft handles), and all kinds of Rubbermaid products. Near the front we found Loofa sponges at $1.99 for the shower or bath and natural sea sponges for applying make-up. The linen selection is good and includes name brand and designer varieties.

Linens'n Things

Annex of Schaumburg
163 W Golf Rd
Schaumburg, IL
(708) 843-1800

T.H. Mandy Fashion Ctr
Downers Grove, IL

Commons of Chicago Ridge
Chicago Ridge, IL

Bloomingdale Court
Bloomingdale, IL

Lakeview Plaza
Orland Park, IL

Southpoint Shop'g Ctr.
Arlington Heights, IL

Oakbrook Terrace
17 West 714 22nd Street
Oakbrook, IL

Cadwell's Corners Ctr
Deerfield,IL

Fashion Square
Skokie, IL

Chestnut Court
Darien, IL

Hawthorn Hills Fashion
Vernon Hills, IL

Meadows Town Mall
Rolling Meadows, IL

Yorkshire Plaza
Aurora/Naperville, IL

Hours vary as to location.

Linens'n Things definitely carries the best for less, 20% to 50% less. Designer and name brands abound including Cannon, Croscill, Laura Ashley, Bill Blass, Mario Buatta, and Adrienne Vittadini. The selection in the store we visited was excellent and we kept running into items we had purchased for more elsewhere. One set we found particularly attractive was the Cannon Royal Family - 250 thread count - Court of Versailles and they had everything including pillow shams, accessory pillows, and duvet covers. The King duvet cover originally $340 was priced at $239.99. On special sale we noticed Wamsutta, 200 thread count, luxury percale sheets. A twin set comparatively valued at $75 was $19.99. Besides the bed and bath linens, they also carry a wide selection of tablecloths, place mats, bath fixtures and all manner of accessories.

114

Lord & Taylor Clearance Center
Town & Country Mall
445 E. Palatine (Palatine and Arlington Hts. Rd.)
Arlington Heights, IL
(708) 259-4211

M-F 10-9 Sat. 10-6 Sun. 11-5

Lord and Taylor operates three clearance centers around the country, one of them in Arlington Hts. in the Town & Country Mall. This center receives past season merchandise from numerous stores in this general section of the country. The clearance price starts between 35% and 40% off the last marked price, and Thursday through Monday some racks are as much as 60% off. The linen selection varies considerably. During the last visit there were only a few comforters while the visit before the entire left back corner was filled with bed linens.
See Also: Women's and Men's Apparel, Children's Apparel, Lingerie, Fashion Accessories

Polo - Ralph Lauren
Lighthouse Place
(See: Outlet Malls)
(219)874-9442

While you can occasionally find a few Lauren linens at Tuesday Morning or T. J. Maxx, it's really fun to see the wide selection all at discount prices at this outlet! In fact the selection is even better than at some department stores. Included are sheets, pillow cases, comforters, shams, decorator pillows, as well as towels, wash clothes, beach towels, etc. Yes, you receive the same polite help in this department as you do in the rest of the store! During sales the prices are really fantastic, but you do have to sort through tables of towels, etc.
See Also: Women's and Men's Apparel, Children's Apparel, Footwear

Private Lives

39 E. Oak St
Chicago, IL
(312) 337-5474

662 W. Diversey Pkwy.
Chicago, IL
(312) 525-6464

3011 N. Clark St.
Chicago, IL
(312) 348-4646

2518 Green Bay Rd.
Evanston, IL
(708) 866-8244

Port Clinton Square
610 Central Ave.
Highland Park, IL
(708) 432-2000

Town Center
Route 83 and Lake Cook
Buffalo Grove, IL
(708) 541-8436

Hours vary as to location.

Private Lives which sells bed and bath linens has several stores in the Chicago area - three in the city. We were told that the Diversey Pkwy store carries the discontinued items (40% to 80% off), the other (Clark St.) does not. The regular discounted prices are the same and they are more than willing to check other stores for merchandise (quickly on a computer) and will even UPS it for NO additional charge! Brand names include Esprit, DesCamps, Laura Ashley, Liberty of London, and Ralph Lauren. The latter is sold at regular retail except for special sales twice a year. There is one hour free parking at the Century Parking Garage with a $20 purchase when visiting the Diversey or N. Clark store. There are several special services available including a custom sewing workroom, in home decorating, bridal registry, monogramming, UPS delivery, and special orders, not to mention the very helpful, patient sales personnel.

Spiegel Outlet Stores

1105 W. 35th St.
Chicago, IL

9950 Joliet Rd.
Countryside, IL

220 S. Waukegan Rd.
Deerfield, IL

1432 Butterfield Rd.
Downers Grove, IL

540 S. Route 59
Naperville, IL

4 Orland Park Pl.
Orland Park, IL

1331 N. Rand Rd.
Palatine, IL

200 E. North Ave.
Villa Park, IL

Gurnee Mills
(See: Outlet Malls)

Hours vary as to location.

Yes, Spiegel also carries linens including pillows, comforters, sheets, pillow cases, towels and various items in the bath shop. At the time of our last visit J.P.Stevens slightly irregular towels were 50% to 60% off.
See Also: Women's and Men's Apparel, Children's Apparel, Lingerie, Fashion Accessories, Footwear, Furniture, Housewares

---

Notable: Do your homework: Linens
Buying the best for less implies that one is aware of what the "best" really is. Take time to educate yourself before rushing out to shop. Take sheets for example. The best are the softest (a high thread count) and most durable (long cotton fibers). Go for at least 250 threads per square inch and a quality cotton such as Pima or, even better, Egyptian, and if not 100% cotton, which needs to be ironed, at least a "natural blend" which is 60% cotton/40% polyester.

Tuesday Morning
Finley Sq. Mall
1524 Butterfield
Downers Grove, IL
(708) 620-0445

F&M Bldg.
840 Roselle
Hoffman Estates, IL
(708) 884-8964

The Landings
16801 Torrence Ave
Lansing, IL
(708) 895-9525

Liberty Mill Plaza
904A Milwaukee Ave
Libertyville, IL
(708) 816-3635

Market Meadows Ctr
1241 Naper Blvd
Naperville, IL
(708) 420-0223

Brookside Plaza
Waukegan & Il. Tlwy
Northbrook, IL
(708) 205-9967

Sunrise Plaza
15641 S 94th Ave
Orland Park, IL
(708) 403-3020

4335 W Oakton
Skokie, IL
(708) 674-2468

80th Place Plaza
20 W. 80th Place
(1 block north of U.S. 30)
Merrillville, Ind.
(219) 769-7181

The Annex of Arlington
19 W Rand Rd
Arlington Heights, IL
(708) 670-9497

Summer: May-June   Fall: Aug.-Sept
Holiday: Oct.-Dec.   Winter: Feb.-Mar.
(Call for exact dates and hours)
*Note: The Tuesday before each official opening the
store is open from 3-7PM for "special customers" or
"those in the know"! For instance if the opening
day is Thursday May 2,1991- then go the preceding
Tuesday April 30, anytime between 3 and 7 PM. This
is obviously the best time to see and purchase the
new inventory.

Tuesday Morning has 1st quality closeout "gifts"
at 50% to 80% off regular retail. The "gifts" include
a variety of items, but we've always found a good
selection of linens.   The most fun was finding
several Ralph Lauren sheets in blue and white,
with the comforter to match.   That same trip we
found beautiful lace trimmed sheets, pillow cases
and duvet covers.   The bath linens were also
plentiful. However, the quantities are limited and
the merchandise does vary with each new opening.
They are open only four times during the year for a
month or two at a time so it's best to be early for best
selection! (No, it's not just on Tuesdays!) If you find
something you want or need, the savings are great.
See Also: Housewares

Waccamaw Pottery

Meadows Town Mall
1400 E Golf Rd
Rolling Meadows, IL
(708) 806-6105

Village Crossing
5545 Touhy Ave.
Skokie, IL 60077
(708) 675-3595

Gurnee Mills
(See: Outlet Malls)
(708) 855-0480

Naperville (to be announced)

M-F 10-9 Sat. 10-6 Sun. 11-5
(Gurnee Mills 11-6)

Waccamaw Pottery is a huge store which advertises that it "guarantees low prices on large quantities of quality merchandise." They carry linens as well as every manner of housewares. Signs hanging above certain sections advertise additional markdowns from the marked price. Be sure to take a basket near the front as you enter the store-you'll need it !
See Also: Housewares

119

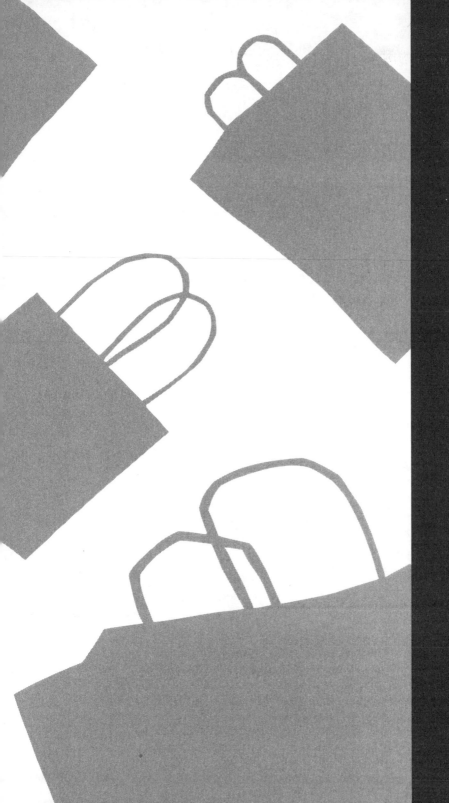

FANTASTIC SALES

Baldwin Warehouse
2615 West Harrison
Bellwood, IL
(798) 544-3200, (800) 339-ORGAN

Want a piano? Try Baldwin's Tent Sale. Check the newspaper or call ahead to discover the date. There are new, used, and reconditioned pianos and new, used organs, floor clocks, and wall and mantel clocks. Location may vary; generally they advertise the week before.

Eddie Bauer Warehouse Sale
Hillside Shopping Center (1991)
Location varies each year

This is the type of sale that you either pitch in, roll up your sleeves, and get to work, or turn around and leave. We stayed and it was worth it! Eddie Bauer moves this annual sale to different cities each year and this was Chicago's turn. They rent space then simply add a row of cash registers and row after row after row of tables. On the tables go cardboard boxes filled with merchandise. I'm sure that once upon a time (perhaps the first few days of the sale) the row labeled women's size small actually contained that, but the system broke down as the sale progressed. Even when we visited, however, at 70% off, there was lots of merchandise. The selection in men's extra large and large was limited, but women's seemed good in all areas. The houseware items were essentially gone, and the selection of linens was diminished. The sale started at 50% off and went down from there. There were tents set up as dressing rooms and this worked well. We picked up large clear plastic bags at the entrance to put our purchases in, then dragged them around until it was time to stand in the check out line which was quite long, but which moved surprisingly well. The sale included Eddie Bauer merchandise from the catalog, stores, and outlets. The markdown came off the marked price which was usually the original price, but not always. There were also a few specials, such as the goose down, ski jacket originally $275, marked to $139, sold at 70% off for $41.70! Check your newspapers for this sale to return in the future and be sure to attend and take your Christmas list!

Ello   Warehouse
500 S. Independence (City Yards)
Rockford, IL

Go to bed early and get a good night's sleep to be in top form for this annual 60% to 90% off Ello Warehouse Sale.   (Ello is a manufacturer of expensive, residential, contemporary furniture.) Did I mention getting up and going at dawn? We heard the line started forming at 5 AM - for those who weren't already there asleep in their lawn chairs, that is!   We also heard that one person offered another $500 for his in-the-front spot in line. We also suspect dealers were there. Yes, it's a fantastically good sale, so if there's something you really want, it's worth the effort - it's kind of fun too! The sale was advertised as being two days, Sat., June 2, 1990 from 9-4 and Sun., June 3, 1990 from 10-1 (essentially the same in 1991), but from what I saw, most items were sold the first hour. They open the doors on time and people start filing in - slowly. It took us fifteen minutes to make it to the door (we lined up at 8:30) and several more minutes to wind around and climb the stairs. Next the decision - left or right?   We turned left and that was the right decision for what we wanted - a table. (Bedroom furniture was to the right.) First we passed a whole grouping of chairs - several people were out of line milling through them but we decided to go on (How do we pick out chairs before we get a table?). We passed wall units and entertainment centers placed along the walls and, presently, various dining tables and chairs and cocktail tables. The sale includes surplus inventory, discontinued models, samples, showroom samples, cancellations, and some items imported from Italy. We spotted what appeared to be a small enough table. I whipped out the tape measure and it was 42" - the maximum size, with four gorgeous cream lacquer chairs, but my husband wasn't sure - he was taller and thought maybe up ahead... I vacillated wanting a smaller size, but the chairs maybe...only $60.00 each. We decided to join the line and keep moving - mistake if we really wanted the set. We learned several things at this our initial Ello sale. Number one, you get one chance at something, no turning around (remember hundreds of folks are pouring in behind you). Secondly, if you want something, stay with it and check the white slip to see how many are available or if this is it - you're not supposed to remove the white copy, you're supposed to wait for a sales clerk to come by and write it up. People did pay attention to each others' claims of ownership - a good thing too. Finally, we decided the absolute best buys might have been on the individual marble tops, glass tops, and mirrors that we weren't looking for and didn't see the first couple times around. Then again, maybe the all marble dining-room table for $400.00 was the best buy. Actually the best buy or bargain is the one you need, want, and can afford. Know what that is, but be prepared for a lot of temptations!

Filene's Basement
State and Madison   Gurnee Mills
Chicago, IL   Gurnee, IL
                          (See: Outlet Malls)
One Schaumburg Place
Schaumburg, IL
Hours vary as to location.

Filene's Basement, headquartered in Boston and famous throughout the Northeast, has arrived in the Chicago area. Noted as the original off-price store, Filene's merchandise comes from manufacturers' and designers' overruns or canceled orders and buyouts from major stores. As excited as we get over the return of bargain basement shopping (Filene's style), we look forward even more to the famous fantastic sales! Look for special sales such as bridal, suits, and end-of-season, then get there early and join the frenzy.

See Also: Women's and Men's Apparel, Fashion Accessories

Institute of Business Designer's Auction
Merchandise Mart
(312) 527-0800

The annual Institute of Business Designer's Auction held in the Merchandise Mart consists of Merchandise Mart showroom samples of first quality office furniture and includes items such as sofas and coffee tables which might be suitable in homes as well. If you need office furniture, you may get lucky here. Many items are sold for 50% to 90% off. Previewing time varies and may include special enticements such as the red tag sale, whereby the selected items drop 5% per half hour. An ad is placed in the Tribune approximately a week before the auction (held Aug. 10, 1990 and Sept. 13, 1991). If you want more lead time, call IBD and either request the date or to be put on the mailing list. Admission in 1991 was $7.00 which included sandwiches. Auction items included a Steelcase context workstation, A. I. Corbusier sofa, Bernhardt Seating, Vecta lounge seating and desk chairs, Lundstead end tables, and much more!

Marshall Field's Warehouse Sale
4000 West Diversey at Pulaski
Chicago, IL
(312) 202-6904

Marshall Field's legendary Warehouse Sale occurs about four or five times a year. They run newspaper ads on the Thursday before and post signs on the warehouse. If you want advance notice or more information, call. They plan the sale about a month in advance. The sale includes furniture (5th floor) as well as household items (1st floor) such as flatware, china, linens, bedding, electronics and appliances. Check the ad for specific merchandise, then plan your strategy with your family or friends! "Shopping sleds", heavy cardboard containers with attached straps, can be centrally located with one person in attendance, while others practice the "shop and dump" technique. Some areas such as flatware and china can be incredibly busy for the first couple hours, while others such as furniture and rugs/carpets are calmer. The accepted method to obtain furniture is to sit on the piece waving your hand frantically for a clerk. Needless to say there are bargains galore, but be aware not everything is reduced to the bone. There are no mail or phone orders and all sales are final. There is a charge for delivery.

Mart Sample Store
St. James Crossing
(5 Min.So.of Oakbrook Shopping Ctr.)
818 E. Ogden Ave.
Westmont, IL. 60559
(708) 789-8155

M,TH 10-9 T,W,F 10-6 Sun.11-5

In July (call or get on the mailing list for the exact days) the Mart Sample Store has its famous Red Tag sale when selected pieces are up to an additional 50% off. I purchased a Wolf cream leather arm chair for the red tag price of ¢375, previously $495, originally $975. Sometimes other show rooms add their merchandise to the sale and in July 1991, an extra storefront was rented for the overflow! Allow yourself enough time for this event as you need to look carefully and your eyes have trouble taking it all in the first time around!
See Also: Furniture

North   Shore   Designer   Mart
6160 Oaktown Street
Morton Grove, IL
(708) 965-6710

The Designer Mart, a division of Carol Home Furnishings, has a showroom at 6949 Dempster which operates year round, but twice a year they open their warehouse on Oaktown Street to the public for a few days for clearance sales. When we visited, the selection of contemporary pieces was very good. There were also accessories including lamps, vases, and artwork. An assortment of bed spreads and dust ruffles was marked 50% off.

The   Shell   Game   Ltd.
1444 Old Skokie Rd.
Highland Park, IL
(708) 831-4480

The Shell Game Ltd. is a manufacturer of fashion accessories. Approximately three times a year they hold sales at the factory on Old Skokie Rd. The sales are open to the public, consist of salesmen's samples, and occur usually in April, July and December. The days, and possibly even the months, will vary so check Material World in the Tribune or look for an ad in the Pioneer Press.

Toms-Price
303 E Front St.
(3 blks. N. of Rt. 38, 3 blks. E of Main St.)
Wheaton, IL
(708) 668-7878
M &Th. 9:30-9   T,W, F, S 9:30-5:30   Sun. 12-5

Toms-Price has THE sale the first week in November for one week. This is the famous, camp out the night before, bring the whole family kind of sale that you prepare for by checking out the goods a week or so in advance, deciding what you want, and assigning members of the family to a specific piece each is to find and purchase. The sale includes all floor samples, accessories included, and the entire store is cleaned out!! The store hires approximately thirty extra salespersons for the event. Delivery is available.

See Also: Furniture

Village Set

757 Central	4116 Dempster
Highland Park, IL	Skokie, IL
(708) 433-8922	(708) 679-5561
M-Sat. 10:30-5:30	Closed Sun.

Sign the mailing list at The Village Set so that you know when the end-of-season sales begin. We were there the last week in July and the sale merchandise had just received its final markdown. With 50% to 80% off top drawer designer clothes, we wanted to buy it all! Nancy W. purchased a gorgeous, navy blue, St. John type knit, City Short set for $75 from hundreds. We were so excited that later we checked out the other location and this time I found the City Short outfit - white linen shorts with a bright block colored baseball jacket. It was mine for $75 from $225.

See Also: Specialty Stores

Weber
200 East Daniels Rd
Palatine, IL

Weber grills, etc. are manufactured in Palatine, IL. Once a year they hold a fantastic sale with savings up to 50% on seconds, discontinued items, and overstocks. Paying cash earns you an extra 5% off. This sale is traditionally held on the 4th weekend of June, but call to confirm and ask directions or check for ads in the newspaper.

T he stores in this section are noteworthy for reasons beyond price. They manufacture or supply unique products, building products, or provide special services, or are simply outstanding in their category. While some offer lower prices, others do not.

SPECIALTY STORES

Architectural Artifacts
3759 N. Ravenswood Ave
Chicago, IL
(312) 348-0622
Tu-Sat 10-5 and by appointment

Architectural Artifacts, operated by Stuart Grannen and his sister Sheila, contains exactly that - all nicely displayed and tagged. The tags both identify the item (sometimes we're not sure), and give the price. To enter this wonderland, however, is another story. We discovered that the merchandise rides the elevator in this old warehouse and people walk up the narrow, tightly winding, open spiral staircase! Once inside there are approximately 10,000 sq.ft. of 19th and 20th century items such as mantels, light fixtures, ceramic tile, pedestals (one pub table base was priced at $165), terra cotta statuary, and a large collection of old, wooden hand tools (block planes ranged from $12 to $50). If you're looking for interesting artifacts, or that one special item, this may be the place! If you're interested in being educated, watch for the Grannens' periodically staged exhibits such as the show entitled "Lost Chicago Found".

Architectural Impressions
1730 Algonquin Rd
Arlington Heights, IL
(708) 634-3909
M-F 10-5 Sat. 11-4

Architectural Impressions creates architectural products and has a complete design service. They specialize in fireplace mantels and surrounds, crown moldings, ceiling medallions, architectural paneling and cabinets, columns, domes and niches, door and window trim, and custom millwork. While they work with builders and designers, they will also work with the general public. Their showroom is beautifully done and shows examples of many of their products. Maria Piper, the Account Representative, was extremely helpful and informative. Yes, they will install.

B. Leader & Sons, Inc.
2042 N. Halsted
Chicago, IL
(312) 549-2224
M 10-4:30   T-Th 10-5:30   Sat. 11-5:30
Closed Sun.

Located next to Les Plumes (have dinner there sometime), in the popular Sheffield neighborhood area of Lincoln Park, B. Leader & Sons creates custom jewelry on the premises out of primarily 14K gold. Many fine pieces are on display as well. They carry Mont Blanc, and do appraisals and repair work. Parking can be a problem, but resist the temptation to park in a no parking zone as tickets are $25.00.

Cabinet Wholesalers
Park Place Shopping Place
1377 North Rand Road
Palatine, IL 60067
(708) 705-6666

Cabinet Wholesalers advertises 50% off retail and runs promotions every week. (Mike indicated that more discount might be available if paid in full) They carry laminate, particle board, all wood cabinets, and custom cabinets which are available in both laminate and wood. They will field measure and will price the job both with or without installation. (They estimate that they install probably 1/3 of the cabinets sold.)

Chicago Antiques Center
Leslie Hindman Auctioneers building
215 W. Ohio St.
Chicago, IL
(312) 268-4083
T-S 10-5 Sun 12-5

The Chicago Antiques Center is a collection of twelve unique booths displaying quality art and antiques located on the fifth floor of the Leslie Hindman Auctioneers building. The merchandise runs the gamut from antique lace and linens, to English, French and American furniture and accessories, to fireplace mantels and bronze figures. Dealers include Ascot Antiques, Linda Moscow; Antique Accessories by Joyce, Joyce Goldman; Canterbury House, Joan Gifford; Dale Gillman & Co., Dale Gillman; Georgette Antiques, Georgia Burnett; Kazan Antique Rugs, Robin Oberlander; L'Angleterre, Mary Ellen Marlas; Oriental Decor, Valerie Bennett; Salvage One, Leslie Hindman and Peter Early; and Sandcastle Interiors, Karen and Molly Ellwood. The center was designed by Mark Knauer and is run by Mary Ellen Marlas.

City Lights by Crest
363 W. Erie St.
Chicago, IL 60610
(312) 943-0911
M-F 8:30-5:30 Sat. 9-4

Besides the vast array of lighting fixtures on display at the River North City Lights by Crest (ARTS 1991 Lighting Showroom of the year), this location also has a Lighting Effects Center. In the Center different types of lighting such as halogen, fluorescent and incandescent can be compared. A wall controller is shown which produces four different "scenes" for dining pleasure. Placement of recessed lighting and the resulting effect is demonstrated as well as different styles of cans.

Outdoor lighting is included in a separate lab. The
Center is definitely a learning experience and
worth the trip, especially if you're building or
remodeling. Lighting consultants are available to
go over plans or consult in your home (Chicago
area). Watch for the Ribbon Sale in June when
floor samples are sold at discount - at other times
discount is only to the trade.

Community Home Supply
3924 N. Lincoln
Chicago, IL
(312) 281-7010
M 7-8   T,W 7-6   Th 7-8   F 7-6   S 8-5
Sun. closed

While your plumber gets the largest discount at
Community Home Supply, you can get one too. The
percentage varies with the item. Larger discounts
are available on closeouts or special sale items such
as the Athena Jacuzzui on the floor when we visited
- $1800 from $3300. Occasionally they re-do their
show room and sell all the displays! Community is
one of THE distributors of plumbing supplies and a
visit here is really a treat. The selection is fantastic
- if you're building, it's a must visit.

Creative Mirror Designs
62 West Lake St.   3200 West 95th St.
Addison, IL 60101   Evergreen Park, IL
(708) 543-1166   (708) 423-7620
M-F 9-9 Sat. 9-5   M, Th. 10-9
Sun. 11-5   T,W, F 10-6
                          Sat 9-5 Sun. 11-5

Creative Mirror Designs concentrates on custom
work with mirrors and has available a photo album
of numerous actual jobs that they have completed.
In their showroom they also have numerous
attractive displays, including not only examples of

their custom mirroring, but also unique accessories, a large selection of mirrors, and home furnishings such as tables of glass and acrylic. The articles vary (they do various parade and model homes) and are discounted approximately 25%, more when on sale. When we visited, a free standing full length mirror was on final sale for $199.95 from their price of $495.00, regularly $575.00. When you visit, ask for their free brochure of creative designs "The Magic of Mirrors."

The Electric Outlet
3343 North Clark
Chicago, IL
(312) 348-9911
M,Th. 12-8   T,W,F,S 10-6   Sun. 12-5

Located in the fun 3300 Block of N. Clark Street (a block which includes the Antique Mall, Loomcraft, Hubba Hubba-vintage clothes and jewelry, and Coffee Chicago and the Organic Theater), The Electric Outlet is Crest Lighting's outlet and discounts range from 30% to 75%. We saw fixtures including outdoor lights (a brass carriage type was $45), some chandeliers, and a range of lamps including halogen. They also had a few fans, clocks, and accessories. Merchandise is always coming in so the selection varies. They run monthly specials and at the time of our visit decorator table lamps were $69.95.

Eye on Design
35 South Washington Street
Hinsdale, IL
(708) 986-5228
M-Sat. 9-6

Eye on Design is a collection of experiences housed in small rooms. There's a bead room on the walls of which there are thousands of beads and, in

the center, a large table often surrounded by
individuals who have come to learn how to make
necklaces (No charge except for materials). There's
also a two room museum and seven other rooms
filled with objects, clothing, and jewelry from W.
Africa, China, Peru, Indonesia, Guatemala,
Afghanistan and Mexico. While Lavinia Tackbary
"minds the store", 100 runners travel the world for
her. She refers to them as "traders of the lost art."
While prices are not equal to what you'd expect in a
Chicago gallery, they're not inexpensive.

Gatherings/Faith's   Lacery
89 W. Main St.
West Dundee, IL
(708) 428-0300
M-S 10-5

Gatherings occupies the front of the store and
consists of country type home accessories such as
pottery lamps with coordinating shades,
reproduction home spun fabrics, tableware, and
linens. A six foot handwoven table runner was
$21.95.

Faith's Lacery is located in the back of the store
and includes one of the area's largest selections of
lace curtains - a great many of them attractively
displayed. Pillow shams and bedding are made to
order and some table coverings are available.
Imported laces come from Liechtenstein, the
Netherlands and Scotland. Prices vary but seemed
reasonable. A 70 X 72 balloon type shower curtain
made from 100% poly lace was priced at $58.00.
Parking is available on the side of the building as
well as in the front on the street.

Industrial Revolution
856 W. Belmont
Chicago, IL
(312) PLASTER
Daily 11-8

If you're looking for plaster bases this is the place! The Industrial Revolution carries a wide assortment of columns, gargoyles, and Art Deco, for, according to the owner, Mark Thomas, 50% off normal retail. Prices appeared to range from $20.00 to $275.00. A column 26" high and approximately 16" across was $122.50 unfinished. Materials and help for finishing are available, although, according to the salesman, a cheap flat latex house paint does an excellent job!

J & D Bath-Whirlpool Outlet
2730 N. Elston
Chicago, IL
(312) 252-6886
M-Sat. 9-5 or by appointment

If they happen to have it, the price will be right! The recently opened J & D Bath-Whirlpool Outlet, warehouse style, carries overruns in vanities, sinks, whirlpools, and some starter kitchen cabinets. They had some good looking pedestal sinks - a Laufen black one for $125. Gerber toilets were $99. Delivery is available. (J stands for Jordan Furlett, the President and D for Douglas A. Denning, the Vice President.)

Jay Robert's Antique Warehouse Inc.
149 W. Kinzie St.
Chicago, IL
M-S 10-5

Jay Robert's Antique Warehouse Inc., located a stone's throw from the Chicago Merchandise Mart, has a convenient parking lot right across the street ($6.00 minimum during the week). They have 50,000 sq.ft. of fine antiques from around the world. As we entered, after being buzzed in, we were informed there was 20% off the marked price. Each item is priced and there were some we wished were identified. The staff, however, is knowledgeable and is quite willing to help find or to discuss items. They were also willing, up to a point, to discount beyond 20%. A cast iron, English pub base, which had been sandblasted and polished, sold for $750 from $1050. We saw beautiful mantels, stained glass, various gray cast iron pieces, English pine, etc. The pieces are beautiful and priced accordingly.

Notable: Athletic Cut for "Hunks"

Entering the main stream are suits labeled athletic cut to fit the physique of professional and weekend athletes - those whose silhouette includes broad shoulders and trim waists. The drop (difference between jacket size and pants size), which normally is 6 inches, in an athletic cut is 8 inches or more. Instead of a 42 jacket being teamed with a 36 pant, you'll see 34 or even 32 pants. Going even further are jackets designed for larger biceps, with more room under the arms, and bi-swing backs with pleats that unfold. Pants likewise have fuller legs and seats to accommodate all those muscles. Check these designers - Jones New York, Evan-Picone and Pierre Cardin for suits with an 8 inch drop and Giorgio Armani, Hugo Boss, JAII by Joseph Abboud and V2 by Versace for a good V-shaped fit. Also check out Brooks Brother's Wardrobe Program which allows one to purchase suit jackets and pants separately.

Krasny's
2829 N. Clybourn Ave.
Chicago, IL
(312) 477-5504
M-F 9-6   Sat. 9-5   Closed Sun.

Krasny's, a restaurant supply store open to the public, isn't going to save you a bundle on kitchen supplies, nor will you find unique, decorator items. What you will discover, however, is an excellent selection of glassware, lots of various sized pots and pans (some huge and difficult to find elsewhere), paper products, and a wide range of cooking utensils which we enjoyed looking through - especially when Bob spotted the heavy metal whisk he needed for his Cajun cooking!
See Also: Housewares

Marble Supply International
901 W. Division St.
Chicago, IL
(312) 787-0990
M-F 8-5:45 S 10-4:30 Sun. 11:30-4:30

Marble Supply International carries an assortment of natural stone - a wide selection of marble and granite. The savings is approximately 20% on cut-to-order pieces and more on remnants and sale items. Bob and I went directly to the lowest priced irregular mini slabs. The granite sold for $60 per sq. ft. and the marble for $35. The piece of granite we selected for $90 was almost rectangular with a polished face and broken sides. If you don't want to chisel away on it yourself, they will custom fabricate pieces to order. If you simply want a finished top or base, there were stacks to choose from. We saw table tops of various sizes and shapes, some bases, a few complete tables, as well as samples of counter tops and fireplace surrounds. If you don't find exactly what you want, they offer custom design service and will field measure.

Office Max

E. Townline Rd.	S. Main at Roosevelt
Vernon Hills, IL	Lombard, IL
(708) 918-9700	(708) 916-8668

Cress Creek Square   Village Crossing Shpg.
Ogden Ave. at Royal St. George   W. Touhy Ave.
Naperville, IL   Niles/Skokie, IL
(708) 717-7571   (708) 647-6888

Remington Plaza   Fretter Plaza
N. Roselle Rd. at Golf Rd.   S. Cicero Ave.
Schaumburg, IL   Bedford Park, IL
(708) 884-8010   (708) 496-8211

North Riverside Mall   Brickyard Mall
W. Cermak Rd.   W. Diversey Ave.
North Riverside, IL   Brickyard, IL
(708) 447-0007   (312) 622-8080

Bloomingdale Court Ctr   Deerbrook Mall
W. Army Trail Rd.   Waukegan at Lake Cook
Bloomingdale, IL   Deerfield, IL
(708) 307-6400   (708) 498-9590

1381 N. Rand Rd. at Dundee Rd.
Palatine, IL   Forest Plaza
(708) 705-7605   Rockford, IL

Hours vary as to location

Office Max has the most for the minimum. What a place! It's advertised as a "Supermarket-size store featuring thousands of office supply items, furniture and electronics at 30% to 70% savings." They have everything including a catalog - ask for one at the check-out. As you enter grab a circular to check specials and if you can tear your eyes off the merchandise, look up at the signs above the aisles that tell you where items are located (just like grocery signs!) Have fun - what a way to start off the school year or a new business!

Renovation Source Inc.
3512 N. Southport Ave.
Chicago, IL
T-S 10-6

Renovation Source carries salvaged pieces such as doors and fireplace mantels; reproduction goods including hardware, bathroom and light fixtures and tin ceilings; and new pieces such as their own line of moldings. We saw racks of spindles (standard $5, large $10, stripped $4 extra), stacks of doors, and bins of molding. A piece of statuary I discovered and liked was the Boy with Turtle marked $295. A ceramic pedestal sink was $398. Everything was priced which we found convenient. Parking is on the street; come equipped with patience and gas!

Salvage One
1524 South Sangamon
Chicago, IL 60608
(312) 733-0098
Tues. -Sat. 10-5

Owned since 1986 by Leslie Hindman of auction house fame, Salvage One is the repository of the Midwest's largest collection of architectural artifacts. It is a source for stained and leaded glass, exterior light fixtures, brass doorknobs, decorative wrought-iron, fireplace mantels, molding, marble sinks, etc. - all contained in the 70,000 sq.ft., five floor warehouse. It's self serve and you can forage for days. Besides matching existing woodwork or locating a piece of Chicago history, you can now order customized iron furniture which Salvage One has begun fabricating from its salvaged iron fragments.

Tender Buttons
946 N. Rush Street
Chicago, IL 60611
(312) 337-7033
M-F 10-6   Sat. 10-5:30   Closed Sun.

Button, Button, who's got the button? Tender Buttons that's who. And they're beautiful buttons - lining all four walls. From novelty to vintage to sterling silver and gold plate - even Chanel look-a-likes. Monogrammed Blazer buttons come in 23K gold plate, silver or pewter finish and run $6 for large and $5 for small. There is also a great selection of cuff links.

Variations Inc.
3403 N. Ridge Avenue
Arlington Hts., IL
(708) 398-7007
M-F 9:30-5 Sat 9-2

After weaving around and behind a series of small buildings, we eventually discovered Variations Inc. Not knowing which door to enter, we ended up walking through the manufacturing plant - stopping all work in progress! One begins to understand the 50% savings Variations can offer on its custom laminated furniture and cabinetry - residential or commercial. On display was a multi-section entertainment center for $2400 with rounded corners, brass trim and space for built in speakers, lights, and a section of glass shelves. They can do any look in laminate, and will match wood grain. Fax or bring in a sketch, pictures of what you want, or take advantage of their custom designing. They also work in Corian.

141

Village Set

757 Central	4116 Dempster
Highland Park, IL	Skokie, IL
(708) 433-8922	(708) 679-5561

M-Sat. 10:30-5:30   Closed Sun.

Need a special occasion dress? Go to the specialist, Village Set, winner of the Apparel Industry Board's The Best Retailer Award in 1991. Besides literally hundreds of cocktail dresses and long gowns (stored in the stockroom, just ask), both locations also carry designer daywear and sportswear. Labels include Escada, Bob Mackie, Anne Klein's A Line, and a variety of Chicago designers. Prices for eveningwear range from a couple hundred to thousands. Alterations are available. Before departing take a careful look at the accessories and sign the mailing list to learn of special events and sales.
See Also: Fantastic Sales

The Wallpaper Shop

205 W Goethe (corner of Wells & Goethe)
Chicago, IL
(312) 280-7696

The Wallpaper Shop, a division of Chicago Interior Design Center, has been selling retail for only a short time now; formerly only to the trade. They carry wall coverings, window coverings, carpet, and ceramic tile. Downstairs you will find "average" price papers, carpet, and tile; and upstairs, window treatment displays and high end papers as well as custom papers. They carry the higher end lines of Schumacher/Waverly including the National Trust for Historic Preservation and Archetonic including Earth, Wind and Stone. If they don't have it, they will do the research and get it for you! They also have periodic 30% off sales.

Wallaby   Station
2756 N. Racine   (Racine at Lincoln Ave. and Diversey
Parkway)
Chicago, IL
(312) 883-4477
M, Th 10-8   T,W, F 10-6:30   Sat. 9:30-5:30
Closed Sun.

Wallaby Station sells clothing for the shorter
man (5' 8" and under). Deriving the name from that
of a small kangaroo, Wallaby's, however, goes one
step beyond simply selling short. Everything about
the store is smaller including the chairs and
salesmen. All this plus an atmosphere of tradition
and elegance! They carry short lengths in sizes 34-
52, extra short in 34-44, and short-portly in 40-54.

OUTLET MALLS

Factory Outlet Centre
7700 120th Avenue
(On I-94 and Hwy. 50(Kenosha/Lake Geneva
exit#344)
Kenosha, WI 53142
(414) 857-7961

January-June M-F 9:30-6 Sun 11-5
July through December M-F 9:30-8 Sun 10-6

The Factory Outlet Centre consisting of approximately 110 stores with factory direct savings up to 85% off retail was a pleasant surprise. Located just minutes from Lakeside Marketplace which discounts designer merchandise, I imagined that this mall would cater more to middle of the line shoppers, which it does, but we also found some really outstanding shops here - it's definitely worth the time and effort to sort them out. While the Centre is huge, it's organized in four phases to make it more manageable. Stop at the information Center and pick up a guide. They also have lockers, strollers, and wheelchairs available. When you're ready to take a break, they have a food court with about any fast food you care to consume, or if you want to escape the mall for lunch, try The Taste of Wisconsin on WI 50 close to the mall. (Be sure to check out the display cases of cheese, sausage and baked goods - a Wisconsin treat.) If you can't face trying to do it all in one day, there are several motels in the vicinity. Just imagine a weekend trip with the whole family to do school or Christmas shopping!

The following is a list of stores in the Factory Outlet Centre having to do with apparel, accessories, footwear, home furnishings, and gifts and luggage. The stores are listed in the first category in which they appear. Omitted are stores dealing in food, toys, hobbies, cards or services. For a complete listing obtain a pamphlet from the Information Center:

Men's and Women's Fashions

Aileen
Barbizon Lingerie
Carole Hochman Lingerie
C.J. Chips
Clothing by Farah
The Company Store
Dress Barn
Fureal Leathers
Gitano
Helly-Hansen
Ideas
Jonathan Logan Outlet
Knits by K.T.
Manhattan Factory Store
Mill City Outlet
Munsingwear
Rainbow Fashions
S & K Famous Menswear
Van Heusen

BG Chicago
Bristol County
Casual Male Big and Tall
Clothes Outs
Cluett Factory Store
C.S.O.
Eddie Bauer Outlet
Gentlemen's Wear-House
Hanes Activewear
Hit or Miss
IZOD/Ship'nShore/MONET
Just My Size
L'eggs, Hanes, Bali
Maternity Wearhouse
Multiples
Newport for Men
Russ Togs
70% Off
Winona Knits

Children's Fashions

Carter's Childrenswear
Kids Ca'pers

Jewelry, Accessories

Enchanted Jewelry
Mitchell Leather Shop
Perfume Boutique
Top of the Line Cosmetics
Whitewater Glove

Julie's Jewelry
New Visions
Socks Galore & More
The Wallet Works

Home Furnishings, Gifts and Luggage

American Tourister
The Brighter Side
Corning/Revere
Farberware
Fieldcrest Cannon
Gift Outlet
Home Decor Outlet
Inscriptions
Loomcraft
The Paper Factory
The Ribbon Outlet
West Bend Company Store
Sony Electronics

Artfare
Chicago Records
Dickens Discount Books
Four Seasons
Fuller Brush Outlet
Great Midwest Craftmarket
Houseware Outlet Store
Lamp and Shade Outlet
Paint and Wallpaper Outlet
Regal Ware Factory Outlet
Welcome Home
World Bazaar

147

Family Footwear

Athletic Shoe Factory　　　　Banister Shoe
Bootery Outlet　　　　　　　Frugal Frand's
LaCrosse Footwear Inc.　　　 Little Red Shoe House
Mid America Shoe Factory Outlet

Factory Outlet Mall　(Old Piano Factory)
401 S. 1st Street　(just off 31)
St. Charles, IL
(708) 584-2009
M-F 10-9　Sat. 10-6　Sun. 11-5

On the banks of the Fox River, in the heart of St. Charles, is the Factory Outlet Mall locally known as the Piano Factory Mall because from 1901 until 1938 pianos were built there. Since 1986 it's housed more than two dozen manufacturers' outlets. It has three floors with an elevator as well as escalators for easy access. The rest rooms and the bakery and cafe (The Upper Crust) are located on the third floor. Savings run 20% to 70%.

Stores:

Corning Factory Store　　　　Factory Card Outlet
The Leather Manor　　　　　 Carter's Childrenwear
Claires Clearance　　　　　　Manhattan Factory Outlet
Top of the Line Cosmetics　　 Houseware Outlet Store
Van Heusen Factory Store　　 Aileen Stores, Inc.
Pfaltzgraff Collector's Center　L'eggs/Hanes/Bali
Gitano Factory Store　　　　　Cape Isle Knitters
Temptations Jewelry　　　　　Bass Shoe Factory Outlet
New England Classics　　　　 danray Inc.
Toy Liquidators　　　　　　　Riverside Antiques
Book Warehouse　　　　　　　Sweat Graphics
Jonathan Logan　　　　　　　Kitchen Collection
The Upper Crust　　　　　　　Chicago Records
Banister Shoe　　　　　　　　American Tourister
Just Pants　　　　　　　　　　What A Deal!
Aunt Mary's Yarns, Needlework, Crafts

148

Gurnee   Mills
6136 Grand Ave.
Gurnee Mills, IL

(Intersection of I-94 and U.S. 132:
Across from Great America)

M-S   10-9   Sun.   11-6

Tired of seeing those tax dollars disappear into Wisconsin and Indiana, Illinois is now competing with what is billed as one of the largest outlet malls in the world - two million square feet of retail space; parking to accommodate over 10,000 cars; fourteen proposed anchor store locations (seven committed as of the opening); and in total 250 shops enclosed under one roof. The owner, Western Development Corporation, expects more than one million visitors each month. Besides the shops, Gurnee Mills has two food courts; two customer service areas which provide   information   as   well   as   shopping conveniences such as parcel pick-up, strollers and wheelchairs; a show court with a full-scale theater; and giant TV screens showing videos. There are strategically placed sitting areas, restrooms and directories along the S-shaped mall with its hardwood floors, staggered storefronts, and colorful graphics. There are also pushcart vendors in the aisles dispensing the latest and greatest. The mall is new, attractive and colorful with discounts ranging from 20% to 70% off retail. In your haste to get inside make sure to note exactly where you parked - besides noting which alphabetical section you're in, try to determine which post you're near. We wish they'd numbered each post as well as lettered it. Unless you've got an incredible amount of time, we'd suggest you park by Filene's Basement, anchor D-1, enter the mall at entrance E, turn left and start with the bottom line of the S which contains several of our favorite stores!

The following is a list of stores (as of the opening) which have to do with apparel, accessories, footwear, home furnishings, and gifts and luggage. Omitted are stores dealing in books/novelties, electronics, food, services, and toys. For a complete listing obtain a pamphlet from one of the Customer Service Areas:

Anchors
Bed, Bath & Beyond
Filene's Basement
Marshalls
Phar-Mor
Sears Outlet
Spiegel Outlet Store
Waccamaw

Children's Apparel
Bugle Boy Outlet
Kidsmart Clearance
Star Baby - The Store

Home Furnishings
Brass Factory Outlet
Famous Brands Houseware
Liberty Green
Old Town Glass Works
Oriental Weavers
This End Up Outlet
Wooden Nail

Men's Apparel
Bigsby & Kruthers
Bugle Boy Outlet
The Casual Male Big & Tall
Garage
Guess
S & K Famous Brands
Van Heusen Outlet
Wemco Factory Store

Accessories/Handbags
Affaire Accessories Outlet
Afterthoughts Outlet
American Tourister
Bentley's Luggage Outlet
Bon Voyage
Claire's Boutique Outlet
Dara Michelle
The Handbag Outlet
Metro Handbags
One Last Thing
Route 66 Off Ramp
Secaucus Handbags Outlet
Topkapi
Whims - Sarah Coventry

Jewelry
Christian Bernard Outlet
The Gold Factory Outlet
Jewelry Outlet
Sparks Jewelers
Stone's Jewelers
Ultra

Shoes
Bally Outlet Store
Banister Shoes
Bostonian Shoe Outlet
Capezio Factory Outlet
Famous Footwear
Fayva
Florsheim Shoe Outlet
9 West & Co. Outlet
Payless Shoe Source
Unisa Outlet

150

Sports

Athlete's Foot Outlet
Champs Outlet
Cory Everson Fitness
Erehwon Mountain Sports
Fan Club Outlet
The Finish Line
National Locker Room
Susan Powter Fitness
Chicago Cubs Sports

Unisex

Aca Joe
Berman's Outlet
Bugle Boy Outlet
Bull Shirts Too
County Seat Outlet
Fitigues Outlet
Guess
Jordache Outlet
Leather Shop Outlet
Merry Go Round Outlet
Oak Leather
Specials by Levi

Women's Apparel

Ann Taylor Clearance
The Answer
Brooks Fashions Outlet
Bugle Boy Outlet
Capers Outlet
Chico's
Cirage
Clothestime
CYA Fashions
Dress Barn Outlet
Etienne Aigner

Guess
He-Ro Group
Lingerie Factory
Mondi
999 Stockroom
No Name Outlet
No Nonsense & More
Scribbles Outlet
Tahari Outlet
Trend Club
Westport Woman

Lakeside Marketplace Outlet Center

11211 120th Avenue
(I-94 North at Exit 347(Highway Q)
Kenosha, WI 53142
(414) 857-2101
Summer M-S 10-9 Sun.10-6
Winter M-S 10-6 Sun.

The Lakeside Marketplace Outlet Center is a collection of approximately 60 factory direct designer outlets. It is being built in Phases with I, II, and III now complete and IV nearing completion. The percentage off retail ranges from 20% to 75% with seasonal sales in February and July. The location is convenient, parking plentiful, and the buildings attractive. There is a centrally located lounge area with rest rooms and one busy restaurant. The mall is open seven days a week with expanded hours in the summer. Plan on a really long day if you attempt to cover the mall totally! If you also plan to shop the Factory Outlet Centre located only a couple exits north on I-94, you may want to spend the night in one of the motels located near the Centre.

Stores:

Liz Claiborne
Crystal Works
Harve Benard
Jindo
Van Heusen
Fenn Wright & Manson
Sassafras
Toys Unlimited
Fanny Farmer Candy
Calvin Klein
J.G. Hook
Evan Picone
Kristina K Outlet
Hensen Lingerie
Gitano
Adolfo II
Jordache Outlet
Tanner Factory Store
Capezio
Osh Kosh
Argenti
The North Face
Madeleine Apparel
Geoffrey Beene
Crazy Horse
Anko Also
Au Pazazz
Brands

Anne Klein
Gilligan O'Malley
Leather Loft
Bass Shoe
I.B. Diffusion
J.H. Collectibles
American Tourister
Maidenform
Royal Robbins
E.J. Plum
Prestige Fragrance
Kenneth Cole Shoes
Jones NY Factory
Kitchen Collection
Benetton
Brass Factory
Cambridge Dry Goods
Just Kids Outlet Store
He-Ro Group Outlet
J. Crew Factory Store
Mikasa
Etienne Aigner
Joan & David
Famous Brands Houseware
Media Man
Linen Mill Outlet
Perfumania

Lighthouse   Place
601 Wabash Street
(Follow the signs off I-94, Exit 34B)
Michigan City, In 46360
(219) 879-6506
Tour Bus and Group Information (219) 874-2915
January and February M-S 9-6   Sun. 10-6
March-December M-S 9-8   Sun. 10-6

In the shadow of a huge cooling tower amongst attractive landscaping is a pleasant group of gray and white clapboard and brick buildings which house approximately 90 stores, a restaurant and an old fashioned ice cream parlour known collectively as Lighthouse Place. This is a clean, well maintained and secured, designer outlet mall with upscale customers who are generally well attired and considerate even during the wildest of sales! After parking in the lot right next to the mall, head for the Visitor's Center - the building with the "lighthouse tower" on top. There you can visit the rest rooms and pick up a Tourist Guidebook which includes a map listing and locating all the Lighthouse shops as well as giving information about other points of interest in the area - for instance The Works which is right next to the mall and features a number of boutiques inside a renovated railroad car manufacturing factory. Lighthouse Place is approximately 60 miles from downtown Chicago and worth the trip!

Stores:

Aileen Outlet	American Tourister
Anko Also	Anne Klein Outlet
B.G. Chicago	Banister Shoe
Bass Shoe Outlet	Benetton
Brands Fashion	Carole Hochman Lingerie
Capezio Shoes	Carter's Childrenswear
Corning/Revere	Crystal Works
Dansk Outlet	Fanny Farmer Candy
Fashion Flair/Izod-Ship 'n Shore	Fieldcrest-Cannon
14 Plus Pizazz	Gitano
Hanes Activewear	Hanes/L'eggs/Bali
Harve Benard	Hathaway Factory Store

I.B. Diffusion	Jaymar Factory Outlet
J.H. Collectibles	Jindo Furs
Jonathan Logan	Just Pants Warehouse
Kitchen Collection	Leather Manor
Maidenform Outlet	Manhattan Factory Outlet
Multiples Outlet	Oneida Silver
The Paper Factory	Pelican's Restaurant
Polo-Ralph Lauren	Royal Doulton
Prestige Fragrance& Cosmetics	Scoops Ice Cream
The Ribbon Outlet	Socks Galore
Sassafras	Ties, Etc.
The Stitchery	Skippy's Cards & Gifts
TrendSetters	Toy Liquidators
The Wallet Works	Welcome Home

The following stores opened in 1991:

Boston Traders	Westport Ltd
Carole Little	Wemco
Stone Mountain	Boston Trader Kids
Adrienne Vittadini	Adolfo
Cape Isle	Jones New York
Geoffrey Beene	Michi
Kristina K.	Aileen
J. Crew	Mrs. Powell/Cinn.
Fragrance World	Bugle Boy
Olga/Warner	Etienne Aigner
Chaus	Country Road
Sassafras	Sweatshirt Company
Jordache	Hickey Freeman
Great Outdoor Clothing	Clifford & Wills
Eddie Bauer	

Milk Pail Village - Factory Outlet Stores
North off I-90 on Rt 25
(708) 742-5043   M 10-6 T-S 10-8 Sun 10-6

Milk Pail Village is as picturesque and quaint as its name implies. In an attractive wooded setting are pretty cream colored buildings with blue trim, and a large red barn which houses the **Craft Barn** and **The Houseware Outlet.** There are also **Farmhouse Shops, Factory Outlet Stores** including **Bass Shoes, Capezio and Leather Manor,** and the **Milk Pail restaurant.**

154

INDEXES
GEOGRAPHICAL, MERCHANDISE, STORE

Geographical Index

Geographics: House Number Map

Chicago is an amazingly easy city to navigate once you learn the system. The whole city is laid out according to a grid wherein a block consists of 100 numbers and 8 blocks equal a mile. To learn the grid first locate the intersection of Madison and State; that's 0,0 with Madison Street as the east-west base line and State as the north-south. Then for every block add 100, or 50 for the few half blocks in the thick of downtown. Michigan Ave. is thus 100 East (Wabash is 50 East), while Washington is 100 North and Monroe is 100 South. These block numbers can be found on most maps - we recommend the pocket size Flash Guide - and the whole system makes it easy to pinpoint an address! Remember two things: the Lake is East and State St. is 0, not Michigan Ave. Since you'll be mainly concerned with North and West, you'll soon memorize what blocks the main streets represent and be able to picture essentially where something is, thus the distance involved, when given an address. Quiz: Where is the Art Institute of Chicago in relation to Bloomingdale's and can we park at Bloomie's and walk to the Museum? They're both on Michigan Ave. so they're 100 E, but the Museum is on Adams which is 200 S, and Bloomingdale's is 900 N. That's 11 full blocks or almost a mile and a half, so wear your tennies if you want to walk!

The outlying stores are indexed as to suburb or city while the Chicago stores are classified as to neighborhood.

157

> ## Geographics: Chicago Neighborhoods
> While some neighborhood areas are clearly defined and various sources actually agree as to boundaries, others are not. Our goal is to indicate a group of stores in reasonable proximity so that you can organize a trip in a given area. Thus, if a store is close to a neighborhood, we probably included it.

Naperville
Dan Howard's Maternity Factory, 9
Habitat, 84
Linens'n Things, 114
Loomcraft, 86
Office Max, 138
Spiegel Outlet Stores, 31, 43, 51, 67, 78, 94, 105, 116
Tuesday Morning, 107, 117
Ulta[3], 69
Waccamaw Pottery, 108, 119

Niles
Dan Howard's Maternity Factory, 9
Linens & Wares, 113
Office Max, 138
Sportmart, 32, 44, 79

North Riverside
Dan Howard's Maternity Factory, 9
Office Max, 138
Sportmart, 32, 44, 79

Northbrook
Jindo, 17
Linens & Wares, 113
Tuesday Morning, 107, 117

Northfield
Lucy's Designer Shoes, 76

Oak Lawn
Dan Howard's Maternity Factory, 9
Loomcraft, 86
Marshalls, 25, 41, 66, 103
Sportmart, 32, 44, 79

Oak Brook
Linens'n Things, 114

Orland Park
Cosmetic Center, 59
Dan Howard's Maternity Factory, 9
Linens'n Things, 114
Loomcraft, 86
Spiegel Outlet Stores, 31, 43, 51, 67, 78, 94, 105, 116
Sportmart, 32, 44, 79
Tuesday Morning, 107, 117

Villa Park
Burlington Coat Factory Warehouse, 5, 38, 73, 112
Spiegel Outlet Stores, 31, 43, 51, 67, 78, 94, 105, 116
Waukegan
Carson Pirie Scott Home Outlet Store, 90
West Dundee
Gatherings/Faith's Lacery, 135
Westmont
Mart Sample Store, 93, 126
Wheaton
Gentry, 14
Toms-Price, 94, 127
Wheeling
Sportmart, 32, 44, 79
Wilmette
Calico Corners, 84
Char Crews, Inc., 98
Dan Howard's Maternity Factory, 9
Winnetka
Chocolate Soup, 39

*

Merchandise   Index

ANTIQUES
Chicago Antiques Center, 132
Jay Robert's Antique Warehouse, 136
Wabash Jewelers Mall, 70

APPAREL-CHILDREN
Burlington Coat Factory Warehouse, 38
Carter's Factory Outlet, 38
Children's Outlet,39
Chocolate Soup,39
Coat Rack,9
Eddie Bauer Warehouse Sale, 122
Filene's Basement, 12
"Just Kids", 40
Lord & Taylor Clearance Center, 40
Marshalls, 41
Morris & Sons Co., 41
Nike Factory Outlet, 42
Oshkosh B'Gosh, 42
Otiswear, 42
Polo - Ralph Lauren, 43
Spiegel Outlet Stores, 43
Sportmart, 44
T. J. Maxx, 45
Upper Half, 45

APPAREL-MEN'S
Apparel Center Shops, 3
Arbetman & Goldbug Inc., 3
Brands Fashion Factory Outlets, 4
Burlington Coat Factory Warehouse, 5
Buy-a-Tux, 6
Calvin Klein, 6
Chicago Fur Mart, 7
Chicago Fur Outlet-"Home of the furry godmother", 8
Coat Rack, 9
Eddie Bauer, 10
Eddie Bauer Warehouse Sale, 122
Eisenstein Clothing Co., 11

APPAREL-RESALE

APPAREL-WOMEN'S

BUTTONS
Tender Buttons, 141

CABINETS
Cabinet Wholesalers, 131
Variations Inc., 95

CHINA/CRYSTAL
Char Crews, Inc., 98
Crystal Works Factory Outlet, 101
Mikasa, 103
Pickard Factory Outlet, 104
Royal Doulton, 104
Tuesday Morning, 107
Waccamaw Pottery, 108

CLEANING SUPPLIES
Fuller Brush Factory Outlet, 102
Edward Don & Co. Outlet Store, 102

COSMETICS
Cosmetic Center, 59
Ulta^3, 69

FABRIC
Calico Corners, 84
CMcE Ltd., 8
Crate & Barrel Outlet Store, 100
Gatherings/Faith's Lacery, 135
Hart's Fabric Mart, 85
Loomcraft, 86
Silk Ltd., 3

FOOTWEAR
Bally Outlet Store, 72
Banister Shoe, 72
Brands Fashion Factory Outlets, 72
Burlington Coat Factory Warehouse, 73
Capezio Shoes, 73
Chernin's Shoes, 74
Eddie Bauer, 75

Eddie Bauer Warehouse Sale, 122
Filene's Basement, 12
Joan & David, 75
Kenneth Cole Shoes, 75
Lori's Designer Shoes and Accessories, 76
Lucy's Designer Shoes, 76
Nike Factory Outlet, 77
Polo - Ralph Lauren, 77
Poseyfisher Inc., 78
Shoe Town, 78
Spiegel Outlet Stores, 78
Sportmart, 79
T. J. Maxx, 80
Unisa, 80
Wolinsky & Levy, Inc., 81

FRAGRANCES
Spiegel Outlet Stores, 68
T. J. Maxx, 69
Ulta^3, 69

FURNITURE
Carson Pirie Scott Home Outlet, 90
Designer Sample Store, 90
Ello Warehouse, 123
European Furniture Warehouse, 91
Hufford Furniture Co., 91
Institute of Business Designer's Auction, 125
Jay Robert's Antique Warehouse, 136
Marshall Field's Warehouse Sale, 125
Mart Sample Store, 126
Office Max, 138
Phoenix Design, 93
Spiegel Outlet Stores, 94
Toms-Price, 94
Variations Inc., 95

FURNITURE-RESALE
Interiors on Consignment, 92

Dansk Factory Outlet, 101
Eddie Bauer Warehouse Sale, 122
Edward Don & Co. Outlet Store, 102
Krasny's, 138
Linens & Wares, 113
Marshall Field's Warehouse Sale, 125
Marshalls, 103
Mikasa, 103
Sassafras, 105
Spiegel Outlet Stores, 105
Tuesday Morning, 107
Waccamaw Pottery, 108

JEWELRY

Anko Also, 58
Anne Klein Outlet, 58
B. Leader & Sons, Inc., 131
Casual Corner Clearance Center, 59
Eye on Design, 134
Filene's Basement, 61
Great Lakes Jewelry, 61
Liz Claiborne Outlet Store, 62
Loehmann's, 63
Lori's Designer Shoes and Accessories, 64
Marshall Pierce & Co., 65
Marshalls, 66
Shell Game Ltd., 127
T. H. Mandy, 68
T. J. Maxx, 69
Wabash Jewelers Mall, 70

LEATHER GOODS

Bally Outlet Store, 59
Leather Manor, 62
Lord & Taylor Clearance Center, 64
Mark Shale Outlet, 65
Mitchell Leather Shop, 66
T. J. Maxx, 69

LIGHTING FIXTURES/LAMPS

City Lights by Crest, 132
Electric Outlet, 134

Store   Index

*************Add This Store!*************

If you know of a store that should be included in the next edition of: **Never Pay Retail: Chicagoland,** please fill out the following and mail it to:

GuideLines
P.O.Box 11051
Rockford, IL 61126-1051
If we use it, we'll give you credit!

Store_____
Address_____
_____
Telephone_____
Hours_____
Comments_____
_____
Your name_____
Address_____
_____

***********BOOK ORDER FORM***********

To order additional copies of
Never Pay Retail: Chicagoland
Send check or money order to:
GuideLines,P.O.Box 11051,Rockford, IL 61126-1051
_____Number of copies @ \$9.95 each   _____
Illinois residents add 6 1/4% sales tax   _____
Shipping and handling   <u>\$2.00</u>
Total Price   _____
Ship to:
Name:_____

Address _____

City_____State_____ Zip Code_____
Thank you!
***********You may copy these forms***********
GuideLine books are available at special discounts for bulk purchases for fund raisers or special promotions. Contact GuideLines at P.O.Box 11051,   Rockford, IL 61126-1051